TAKING CONTROL of Adult ADHD

Proven Strategies to Succeed at Work, at Home, and in Relationships

Planner/Workbook included
2 IN 1

Avoid the ADHD overwhelm...

Before you begin, read!

Let me guess... You enjoyed the'researching the planner' process, but now that you've purchased this fantastic book, you're scrolling and feeling a little overwhelmed as to where to begin? Here's why. To build up the planner, you must use logic... I know, not our favourite duty. But it will be so worth it once everything is in place! Take a big breath; you can do it! I'll guide you through it...

Quick start guide, ADHD style

1. Organizing a new planning system requires convergent thinking - which is a muscle ADHD brains don't flex very often. Go to page 37 of the planner document and read about divergent vs. convergent thinking to understand why your brain is likely overwhelmed in this 'convergent' state right now. Get curious, and stay with me/the process!

2. This is part planner and part growth mindset guided workbook. Look for my tips and advice sprinkled throughout, as well as the one page science explainers aptly called 'Bonus Science-y Tips' on the neuroscience and 'why' behind your ADHD brain. Once you understand why your brain functions the way it does, the everyday gets a lot easier.

3. The templates are grouped by section so you can find them easily, but this isn't the final layout. You can design your planner layout any way you want, it's flexible. Some pages are designed to be used every day, others only once a quarter. And some templates you may not need at all! #ADHDyourway #norules

more tips

Table of Contents

Daily concentration buddy

A note from the creator

Fast brain friends, welcome to a planner designed specifically for your brain.

This digital planner isn't just another ordinary planner with ADHD slapped on the title. It's a framework that's designed by an ADHD brain (mine!) especially for your ADHD brain.

I tried different planners for years, but they never seemed to stay and ended up accumulating dust on my bedside table. Does this sound familiar? I used to think I was bad at following through, but now I realise that most plans are created for neurotypical minds. As a result, I created my own planner. This planner differs from others in that it incorporates tools I created, such as the Hyperfocus Lotus, Div/Con planning, and Symmetry Stress-relief. These portions may seem strange, but they function.

Using the Most Recent Science

I've done several #hyperfocus deep dives into the newest research on ADHD in try to understand my ADHD brain wiring. I wanted to go past the bad stereotypes and show the amazing and creative side of neurodivergence that so much of the world overlooks. I was curious as to how executive functioning deficits may stymie me and what additional assistance would be beneficial to me. I've taken what I've learned from reading dozens of books on neuroscience, behavioural psychology, and emotional intelligence, as well as listening to a million podcasts, and designed an ADHD planner that is solidly founded on the most recent scientific results.

Look for my prompts, guidance, and ideas throughout the book - it's like a growth mindset notebook and productivity calendar rolled into one!

From one neurodivergent to another:

_____

future ADHD

Note: commercial/therapy license not included

Get sh*t done

How to use:

Use these to-do list templates and daily and weekly planners to take the tsunami of 'popcorn' thoughts, life admin tasks, creative ideas, rabbit holes and divergent paths pinging away in your brain and create some order.

Our templates include reward zones, self-care visual reminders, habit prompts and 'leave it for later' brain dumps. Print each page as many times as you need, and use every day or as often or as infrequently as you need! #norules #adhdyourway

JUST IN CASE YOU'RE curious

The science bits

ADHD NEUROLOGICAL TRAIT	OUR PLANNER DESIGN
A GREAT DISLIKE TO UNSTIMULATING TASKS, YET A SIGNIFICANT DESIRE TO DOPAMINE/NOVELTY/FUN	A STRONG AVERSION FOR UNSTIMULATING WORK, YET A STRONG NEED FOR DOPAMINE/NOVELTY/FUN
TENDENCY TO BECOME CAUGHT IN DIVERGENT (CREATIVE) THOUGHT AND NOT MOVE TO CONVERGENT THINKING (LOGICAL)	A BALANCED PLANNING TEMPLATE (THE FIRST OF ITS TYPE) THAT COMBINES TIME LIMITATIONS AND REMINDERS TO KEEP YOU FOCUSED ON YOUR AIM
DESIRE FOR GOOD HABITS, BUT FRUSTRATION RESULTING FROM A LACK OF CONSISTENCY IN HABITS AND DISCIPLINE	REMINDERS FOR HABIT GOAL CHECKBOXES ON EVERY PLANNING PAGE LEVEL: DAILY, WEEKLY, AND MONTHLY (LINKED TO THE GOALS YOU SET IN THE HEALTHY HABITS SECTION)

ADHD + time perception

According to research, ADHD brains see time differently than other people. In fact it is so strange, it has even been nicknamed 'time blindness'. There are two time zones in our neurodivergent world: 'now' and 'not now'. This is frequently because we are so engrossed in an activity that we have no awareness of the passing seconds. We've fallen into a time vortex.

Our 'time blindness' correlates with another ADHD trait, the inability to differentiate between low and high priority tasks. This is due to our proclivity for large picture thinking, creativity, and invention (as well as our aversion of 'boring details').

Consider this frequent ADHD scenario... We'll be cooking in the kitchen when we receive an inspiration for a wonderful new kitchen gadget that hasn't been developed yet but has the potential to improve people's lives due to its brilliance and simplicity. We fantasise at the stove, seeing a warehouse full with this great gadget, consumers buying in droves, money flowing into our bank account, and using our newfound wealth to purchase a new house or automobile. Would we choose for a hybrid or an electric vehicle? Then we smell burning and realise we've lost track of time, and the spaghetti sauce is boiling over and splattering.

Our impression of time influences our deadlines and prioritisation of daily work. Everything appears to be equally vital and urgent to us. It's exhausting to be forced to discern what isn't truly vital, because conscious prioritisation isn't a muscle we often exercise (though we do it unconsciously when we prioritise new business ideations over a well-cooked dinner.) As we try to mull it through, balancing each activity for importance, our irritation tolerance grows and we throw up our hands in overwhelm and assert 'everything is equally vital and must happen this instant'. This is virtually never the case.

6

Divergent thinking is crucial for brainstorming and generating multiple ideas. As someone with ADHD, I often struggle with focusing on a single task or idea, and divergent thinking allows me to explore multiple options and come up with unique solutions. This is particularly helpful when I am feeling stuck or unmotivated, as it allows me to think outside of the box and find new perspectives.

Convergent thinking, on the other hand, is essential for organizing my thoughts and narrowing down my options. As someone with ADHD, I can easily become overwhelmed by the plethora of ideas generated through divergent thinking, and convergent thinking helps me to focus and make a plan of action. This type of thinking also allows me to break down complex tasks into manageable steps, which is crucial for staying on track and completing my project.

Convergent thinking, on the other hand, is essential for organizing my thoughts and narrowing down my options. As someone with ADHD, I can easily become overwhelmed by the plethora of ideas generated through divergent thinking, and convergent thinking helps me to focus and make a plan of action. This type of thinking also allows me to break down complex tasks into manageable steps, which is crucial for staying on track and completing my project.

I have also found that by utilizing both forms of thinking, I am better able to manage my impulsivity and make more thoughtful decisions. By thinking divergently, I am able to generate multiple ideas and options, and then by thinking convergently, I can evaluate and choose the best course of action.

Overall, by utilizing both divergent and convergent thinking, I am able to effectively manage my ADHD symptoms, stay focused and motivated, and achieve success in my projects.

Daily focus friend

DATE:

FOCUS/QUOTE:

SELF-CARE:

TODAY – TIME BLOCKING:

| 5 AM |
| 6 AM |
| 7 AM |
| 8 AM |
| 9 AM |
| 10 AM |
| 11 AM |
| 12 PM |
| 1 PM |
| 2 PM |
| 3 PM |
| 4 PM |
| 5 PM |
| 6 PM |
| 7 PM |
| 8 PM |
| 9 PM |

BORING (BUT NECESSARY) TASKS:

01	
0	
2	

🎉 REWARD TO MYSELF AFTER:

3

DON'T FORGET:

☐ _____

☐ _____

☐ _____

☐ _____

PEOPLE TO RESPOND TO:

☐ _____

☐ _____

☐ _____

LEAVE IT FOR LATER BRAIN DUMP:

HABIT GO

☐ DONE

8

Daily focus friend

DATE:

FOCUS/QUOTE:

TODAY - TIME BLOCKING:

SELF-CARE:

BORING (BUT NECESSARY) TASKS:

01	
0	
2	

🎉 REWARD TO MYSELF AFTER:

3

DON'T FORGET:

- ☐
- ☐
- ☐
- ☐

PEOPLE TO RESPOND TO:

- ☐
- ☐
- ☐

LEAVE IT FOR LATER* BRAIN DUMP:

HABIT GOAL:

☐ DONE

Daily focus friend

S   M   T   W   T   F   S

Remember to stretch, hydrate and get vitamin D!

MOOD:

QUOTE:

TOP 3 PRIORITIES:

☐

☐

☐

WEATHER:

REMINDER TO:

TODAY AT A GLANCE:

TIME:	EVENT:

MIND + BODY:

MINUTES MEDITATING:	
MINUTES STRETCHING:	
MINUTES EXERCISING:	
TOTAL STEPS:	

TASK LIST:

☐

☐

☐

☐

☐

☐

☐

HYDRATION TRACKER:

MEAL TRACKER:

BREAKFAST:	LUNCH:
DINNER:	SNACKS:

TO CALL OR EMAIL:

URGENT:	SOON:

LEAVE 'TIL TOMORROW:

☐

☐

☐

TODAY I AM GRATEFUL FOR:

LEAVE IT FOR LATER BRAIN DUMP:

HABIT GO...

☐

DONE

10

Weekly planner

FOCUS/QUOTE:

ONDAY

JESDAY

EDNESDAY

HURSDAY

RIDAY

ATURDAY / SUNDAY

ABIT FOCUS THIS WEEK:

NAILED IT!

ABIT TRACKING: _____

BORING (BUT NECESSARY) TASKS:

01	
0	
2	

REWARD TO MYSELF AFTER:

3

TO-DO

☐ _____

☐ _____

☐ _____

☐ _____

☐ _____

☐ _____

☐ _____

TASKS I CAN PUSH TO NEXT WEEK:

(1) (2) (3) (4) (5) (6) (7)

Weekly planner

FOCUS/QUOTE:

MONDAY

TUESDAY

WEDNESDAY

THURSDAY

BORING (BUT NECESSARY) TASKS:

01	
0	
2	

REWARD TO MYSELF AFTER:

3

TO-DO

- [ ]
- [ ]
- [ ]
- [ ]
- [ ]
- [ ]
- [ ]

NOTES

HABIT FOCUS THIS WEEK:

NAILED IT!
- [ ]

Weekly planner

FOCUS/QUOTE:

RIDAY

SATURDAY

SUNDAY

NEXT WEEK

BORING (BUT NECESSARY) TASKS:

01	
0	
2	

🎉 REWARD TO MYSELF AFTER: ↙

3

DON'T FORGET

☐

☐

☐

☐

☐

☐

☐

TASKS I CAN PUSH TO NEXT WEEK:

HABIT TRACKING: _____

① ② ③ ④ ⑤ ⑥ ⑦

13

Month overview

Use the flexible boxes below to jot down what's on the agenda each week in the upcoming month.

WEEK OF: / /

HIGH PRIORITY TASKS:
- [ ] _____
- [ ] _____
- [ ] _____
- [ ] _____

WEEK OF: / /

HIGH PRIORITY TASKS:
- [ ] _____
- [ ] _____
- [ ] _____
- [ ] _____

WEEK OF: / /

HIGH PRIORITY TASKS:
- [ ] _____
- [ ] _____
- [ ] _____
- [ ] _____

WEEK OF: / /

HIGH PRIORITY TASKS:
- [ ] _____
- [ ] _____
- [ ] _____
- [ ] _____

HABIT FOCUS THIS MONTH:

NAILED IT!
- [ ]

Do it with dopamine

Things I'm not passionate about but still need to do #adultingwithADHD

	ESSENTIAL TASK TO DO	REWARD AFTER	DONE
1			○
2			○
3			○
4			○
5			○
6			○
7			○
8			○

Get sh*t done days

Boring but necessary tasks:

Boring but necessary tasks:

☐ _____

☐ _____

🎉 REWARD TO MYSELF AFTER:

☐ _____

☐ _____

🎉 REWARD TO MYSELF AFTER:

☐ _____

☐ _____

🎉 KNOCK OFF AND RELAX:

Get it done days

Boring but necessary tasks:

- [ ] _____

- [ ] _____

> 🎉 REWARD TO MYSELF AFTER:

- [ ] _____

- [ ] _____

> 🎉 REWARD TO MYSELF AFTER:

- [ ] _____

- [ ] _____

> 🎉 KNOCK OFF AND RELAX:

Get sh*t done weekends

Boring but necessary tasks:

- [ ] _____
- [ ] _____

> 🎉 **REWARD TO MYSELF AFTER:**

- [ ] _____
- [ ] _____

> 🎉 **REWARD TO MYSELF AFTER:**

- [ ] _____
- [ ] _____

> 🎉 **KNOCK OFF AND RELAX:**

Get it done weekends

Boring but necessary tasks:

- [ ] _____

- [ ] _____

🎉 REWARD TO MYSELF AFTER:

- [ ] _____

- [ ] _____

🎉 REWARD TO MYSELF AFTER:

- [ ] _____

- [ ] _____

🎉 KNOCK OFF AND RELAX:

Divergent vs. convergent thinking

Divergent thinking = creative ideation

Convergent thinking = logical execution

Learning the difference between divergent and convergent thinking, and realising I spend most of my time in divergent thinking mode, changed everything for me. Dr Tamara Rosier explains that children have a natural capacity for divergent thinking, but by adulthood, most neurotypical brains are comfortable in convergent thinking mode. Both convergent and divergent thinking are important, but when we use one more than another, we can get stuck on tasks, either at the ideation phase or the execution phase.

"Divergent thinkers have possibility brains," Dr Rosier says. "Their minds naturally explore and elaborate on ideas, examining what could be."

But ADHD brains have a tendency to stay stuck in the 'divergent thinking' brainstorm stage way too long. Why? Because it delivers opportunities for novelty, experimentation and visualisation - things our brains looove. Exploring a new idea or starting a new project is important, but to meet our goals, we need to move to the 'taking action' phase before we lose interest, and that's where those (dreaded) convergent thinking skills come in.

Like me, you might be wondering - huh? **What is convergent thinking?**

We use convergent thinking to work out the action steps to achieve our goal (after the blue-sky brainstorming phase). There is more grunt work, logic, discipline and persistence required... systemising, categorising, organising with a goal towards clarity and efficiency. It might sound boring, but divergent thinking imagines wonderful possibilities and convergent thinking **actually creates those. They are both crucial steps.**

The following template 'Div/Con Planning' will help you find a balance between divergent and convergent thinking. Set a clear goal that you can visualise and 'feel' when you close your eyes, because this increases your motivation. Set a time limit on how long you'll spend in divergent thinking mode, and when you'll move to convergent thinking. Convergent thinking may tire you out, but keep reminding yourself of your goal and visualising yourself enjoying it to keep your brain on track.

We also have visual exercises to help you move from divergent to convergent in our Unwind Un-mind section.

Div/Con Planning

Find a balance of divergent & convergent thinking as you plan your next project...
eg. your upcoming vacation, birthday party, new home, or re-decorating your bedroom.

1. OUTCOME/GOAL/MY 'WHY':

Plan a holiday somewhere warm where I can relax and switch off from work. I want to zone out, eat delicious food and read a good book.

Be descriptive, and visualise how you'll feel

2. DIVERGENT THINKING BRAINSTORM:

Set a time limit on divergent thinking

Bali for a diving trip

The Maldives?? Too expensive

That sound-healing retreat my colleague went to in Arizona

Do I want friends to come or go alone? Need to find a friend who wants the same kind of holiday as me.

Cheap flights to Spain but I want to do Barcelona when I have the energy to be a tourist. So maybe not for this type of holiday.

Resort style so I can eat out and not have to cook vs. airbnb with kitchen?

TIME LIMIT!

2

MINS/HRS

3. MY DECISION: Resort in Bali where I can stay by the pool all day

4. CONVERGENT THINKING TASK LIST:

What practical steps do I need to take, that will help me achieve my goal?

- [ ] Budget based on priorities, my
- [ ] 'why' Find an all-inclusive
- [ ] resort package
- [ ] Request time off work
- [ ] Book by 15th April
- [ ] Research flights

Book airport transfer

- [ ] Organise house sitter
- [ ] Find passport
- [ ] Change money
- [ ] Pack bags

If you get lost and feel tempted to slip back ir divergent thinking, remember to focus on your goal, visualise how you want to feel, and use th positive feeling to create actionable steps and on track. Your future self will thank you.

Div/Con planning

Find a balance of divergent & convergent thinking as you plan your next project... eg. your upcoming vacation, birthday party, new home, or re-decorating your bedroom.

1.OUTCOME/GOAL/MY 'WHY':

Be descriptiv and visualise how you feel

_____

_____

2. DIVERGENT THINKING BRAINSTORM:

Set time limi divet thin

TIME LIM

MINS/HRS

3. MY DECISION:

4. CONVERGENT THINKING TASK LIST:

What practical steps do I need to take, that will help me achieve my goal?

☐ _____   ☐ _____

☐ _____   ☐ _____

☐ _____   ☐ _____

☐ _____   ☐ _____

☐ _____

☐ _____

If you get lost and feel tempted to slip divergent thinking, remember to focus o goal, visualise how you want to feel, and positive feeling to create actionable step on track. Your future self will thank

Real-life prioritisation

Our ADHD brains find it more difficult to distinguish between the importance of tasks than our neurotypical friends. Small and big things all feel huge, and often overwhelming and insurmountable. Use the Eisenhower matrix to disrupt the catastrophising vice-like spiral of doom and help you prioritise and delegate tasks based on real-world consequences + facts.

do first
urgent + important

do later
important, not urgent

delegate
urgent, not important

eliminate
not important, not urgent

2

In this section:

tips & how it works

Remember stuff

How to use:

Use these trackers and list templates to create calm(er) order in the flood of ideas, books, new faces, media, life admin tasks and rabbit holes you experience daily.

Our templates include focus areas that ADHDers commonly report are prone to forgetfulness: tracking parcels, passwords, D&M conversations with good friends, or 20 half-finished podcast episodes.

JUST IN CASE YOU'RE curious

The science bits

ADHD NEUROLOGICAL TRAIT

DIFFICULTY WITH SHORT TERM MEMORY, LEADING TO FORGETFULNESS, FRUSTRATION AND FINANCIAL CONSEQUENCES COMMONLY TERMED #ADHDTAX

INSATIABLE CURIOSITY AND A THIRST FOR LEARNING ARE COMMON ADHD TRAITS, WHICH IS WHY WE MOVE SO QUICKLY FROM ONE TOPIC OF INTEREST TO ANOTHER, AND HAVE 20 PODCAST EPISODES LEFT UNFINISHED

OUR PLANNER DESIGN

THESE TRACKERS & LISTS ARE DESIGNED TO TAKE THE PRESSURE OFF YOUR BRAIN TO REMEMBER SO MANY TINY DETAILS, SO YOU DON'T LOSE TRACK OF THOSE 9 WIDGETS YOU ORDERED LAST WEEK

UNLIKE OTHER PLANNERS WE ASSUME YOU WILL HAVE UNFINISHED BOOKS/MEDIA, AND CREATED LISTS DESIGNED ESPECIALLY FOR TRACKING INCOMPLETE PODCASTS AND BOOKS (WITH CATCHY TITLES TO ENSURE YOU CAN FIND THEM AGAIN.)

New friends

Never awkwardly forget someone's name again. Yay!

NAME	DATE	LOCATION MET	WE TALKED ABOUT...

D+M tracker

You see your friend and have great D&Ms (Deep & Meaningful chats) whenever you catch up, but find yourself forgetting the details of what you talked about the next time you see them. Use this handy table to keep track of conversations with your nearest & dearest, or as a prompt to send a check-in message.

FRIEND'S NAME	DATE & LOCATION	WE TALKED ABOUT...

#ADHDtax tracker

#ADHDtax is a commonly used phrase on social media now. If you're unfamiliar, it references moments where you forgot something (due to your ADHD brain) and as a result, you lost money or a valuable item. Eg. caught up in your own thoughts while on the train, and leaving your $300 earbuds behind on the train seat

DESCRIBE THE 'ADHD TAX' INCIDENT	STRATEGIES SO I DON'T DO THIS AGAIN

Current hyper-focus

Use this list as a 'brain dump' to jot down books, courses, websites, podcasts, apps & videos you want to consume about your latest obsession, so you can find them later.

TOPIC:

- [ ]
- [ ]
- [ ]
- [ ]
- [ ]
- [ ]
- [ ]
- [ ]
- [ ]
- [ ]

Parcel tracker

Missing mail no more! Get the details out of your brain and onto the page so you remember you have an Amazon package (or five!) coming.

PARCEL/ORDER DETAILS	EST. ARRIVAL	⊘

Cart: the 24 hour rule

Our ADHD brains looove a burst of impulsivity. One minute we're scrolling, the next minute, we're five items deep in an online shopping cart and about to click purchase on $187. Write down those items here and see whether you still feel that burning desire to buy 24 hours later. Your bank account will thank you!

ONLINE STORE	ITEMS IN MY BASKET RIGHT NOW	⊗	✓

Password tracker

WEBSITE / APPS

USERNAME

PASSWORD

WEBSITE / APPS

USERNAME

PASSWORD

WEBSITE / APPS

USERNAME

PASSWORD

WEBSITE / APPS

USERNAME

PASSWORD

WEBSITE / APPS

USERNAME

PASSWORD

WEBSITE / APPS

USERNAME

PASSWORD

WEBSITE / APPS

USERNAME

PASSWORD

WEBSITE / APPS

USERNAME

PASSWORD

WEBSITE / APPS

USERNAME

PASSWORD

WEBSITE / APPS

USERNAME

PASSWORD

Books I started

We love to read 10 books at once, don't we? Note down your current reads here so when you bounce to the next topic of interest, you can pop back to finish anytime.

BOOK TITLE & DESCRIPTION	AUTHOR	✓

Podcasts I want to finish

Who has time to finish podcast episodes when there are so many shiny new podcasts we want to listen to? Our ADHD brains crave stimulation and novelty, and it's quite normal for us to jump between many podcasts episodes in a day, and still retain all the knowledge! It's our special way and hey, often it works. Keep episodes listed here to circle back around to later on.

PODCAST EPISODE TITLE & NUMBER	PODCAST NAME	✓

Assignment tracker

ADHD brains are typically 'time blind', where we have difficulty judging how long things take. We often think in two distinct time frames - either 'now' or 'not now'. If it's 'now, we're totally immersed, and 'not now' means it might as well be years away in our minds! Having visual cues in front of us is especially important - put this list up on the wall or fridge so it's visible.

	ASSIGNMENT/PROJECT	DEADLINE	DONE
1			○
2			○
3			○
4			○
5			○
6			○
7			○
8			○

Create healthy habits

3

In this section:

Self-care assessment wheel

Habit visualisation journal

Quarterly habit planning - structured layout

Quarterly habit planning - journey layout

Habit evaluation

Future projection - habit journal page

Limiting self-belief reframe

all of these templates tie in with the tracking pages in the 'Self-Care' section.

tips & how it works

Create healthy habits

How to use:

☑ Use these templates to evaluate your current balance of habits across 8 core domains: nutrition, relationships, sleep & rest, screen-free time, dental health, exercise, play & curiosity, and mindfulness

☑ Start with an assessment wheel, and use that as a guide for where you need to start habit planning and reflection. Choose habits that align with your personal values and your 'why' to reduce some resistance. Sounds daunting? Don't stress! There are looots of tips and guided prompts through this section! :)

JUST IN CASE YOU'RE curious

The science bits
OUR PLANNER DESIGN

ADHD NEUROLOGICAL TRAIT	
EXTREME EITHER/OR THINKING TYPICAL OF ADHD BRAINS MEANS THAT IF WE MISS A DAY, WE CAN THROW OUT THE WHOLE HABIT TRACKER AND GIVE UP	I'VE DESIGNED TEMPLATES THAT SUPPORT A KINDER, MORE SELF-COMPASSIONATE APPROACH TO 'FALLING OFF THE BANDWAGON' WITH FRIENDLY TIPS & REMINDERS
WE HAVE A BURST OF EXCITEMENT INITIALLY, BUT THEN THAT PETERS OUT MID-WAY THROUGH A PROJECT/GOAL BECAUSE WE LOSE SIGHT OF THE VISION	USE THE HABIT VISUALISATION JOURNAL TO REALLY GET CLEAR ON YOUR WHY AND HOW YOU'LL FEEL WHEN YOU'VE CREATED THE HABIT. THIS WILL KEEP YOU ON TRACK.
TYPICALLY WE RUN WITH A VISION UNTIL WE GET TRIPPED UP BY THE MULTIPLE SMALLER STEPS THAT REQUIRE SUPERIOR EXECUTIVE FUNCTIONING	I'VE INCLUDED GUIDED, STEP-BY-STEP PROMPTS TO HELP YOU CHUNK DOWN YOUR GOALS AND STAY REALISTIC SO YOU HAVE A GREATER CHANCE OF SUCCESS

Self-care assessment wheel

Evaluate how you're tracking on the below aspects of self-care by colouring in the wheel. 1 is lowest care, 10 is highest care. This is a helpful tool as you set healthy habit goals across the next pages.

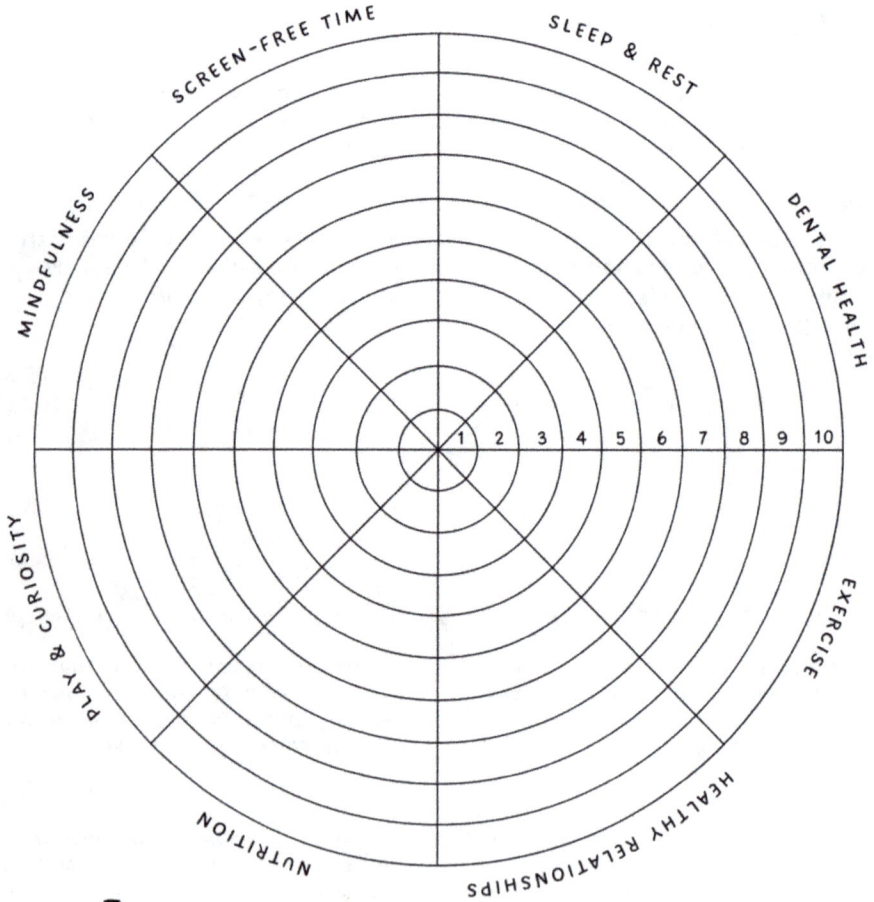

SCREEN-FREE TIME

SLEEP & REST

MINDFULNESS

DENTAL HEALTH

1 2 3 4 5 6 7 8 9 10

PLAY & CURIOSITY

EXERCISE

NUTRITION

HEALTHY RELATIONSHIPS

You can use this wheel multiple times, eg. as bi-annual or annual assessment tool to evaluate how you're tracking against habit & wellness goals.

Which habit do you want to focus on first?

38

ADHD + motivation

lack of

People with ADHD have a lot of drive when it comes to things they are enthusiastic about, but absolutely no motivation when it comes to jobs they are forced to perform or aren't fun. We frequently struggle with habits because we loathe taking action on routine tasks about which we are uninterested. Our drive to accomplish things is tied to our interest, which is normally quite boundless and centred on nuanced, complicated thoughts - therefore basic jobs bore us rapidly. Dr. Russell Barkley, the world's leading specialist on ADHD, believes that ADHD is more about a lack of interest and drive than a loss of attention and focus. He claims that the secret to getting things done is to recognise the emotions at work and either harness or redirect them.

Tamara Rosier's book 'Your brain is not broken' compares it to an emotional 'light switch' function, which means we experience strong extremes in our emotions to activities, much like a light switch on or off, with no shades of grey in between. We'll either dislike or adore something, be entirely uninterested or extremely involved and emotional. Instead of employing our pre-frontal cortex for executive functioning, we rely on our emotional centres in the limbic system and amygdala to push us to execute jobs we don't want to do through generated stress, urgency, and emotion. Sounds familiar?

IWe may use our above-average imaginations to boost our drive and tenacity in dealing with the routine. Our brains are capable of vividly seeing future events in remarkable detail, even precisely forecasting the vast array of emotions we may experience. And how we feel inspires us.

Assume we wish to perform a multi-day hike up Machu Picchu that requires altitude training. We may use the Habit visualisation journalling form (on the next page) to visualise every detail of the trip, including how we will feel strolling amid the clouds. Doing that visualisation before scheduling our vacation, and doing it on a regular basis, will help us re-calibrate. When we lack desire to wake up early and workout, we may utilise these powerful visualisation techniques to remind ourselves of the final objective... our why. This stimulates our limbic system and provides us with a short rush of dopamine, as well as a powerful hit of determination to keep going.

Journal of Habit Visualization

If you really want a habit to stick, you've got to align your 'why' with behaviour, and work out from a clear vision of how it will feel to have achieved this goal.

MON   TUE   WED   THU   FRI   SAT   SUN

○   ○   ○   ○   ○   ○   ○

DATE:

Visualise how you'll feel when you have consistently and successfully created this new habit. Write (in detail) about why it will be amazing for you.

_____

_____

_____

_____

_____

_____

_____

_____

_____

_____

_____

_____

_____

_____

_____

_____

_____

_____

_____

_____

_____

_____

Quarterly habit planning

Structured layout)

REFLECTION ON HOW I WENT LAST QUARTER:

DATE:

_____

_____

_____

_____

THINGS I ALREADY DO PRETTY WELL:

NUTRITION GOALS THIS QUARTER:

MY BIGGEST SELF-CARE GOAL THIS QUARTER:

_____

_____

WHY DO I WANT TO SET THIS SELF-CARE GOAL?

This is crucial!)

_____

_____

HABITS THAT HELP MEET THIS

GOAL: 01

2

3

4

5

5

WHAT IS ACTUALLY REALISTIC:

Pick 3 self-care habits

☐

☐

☐

41

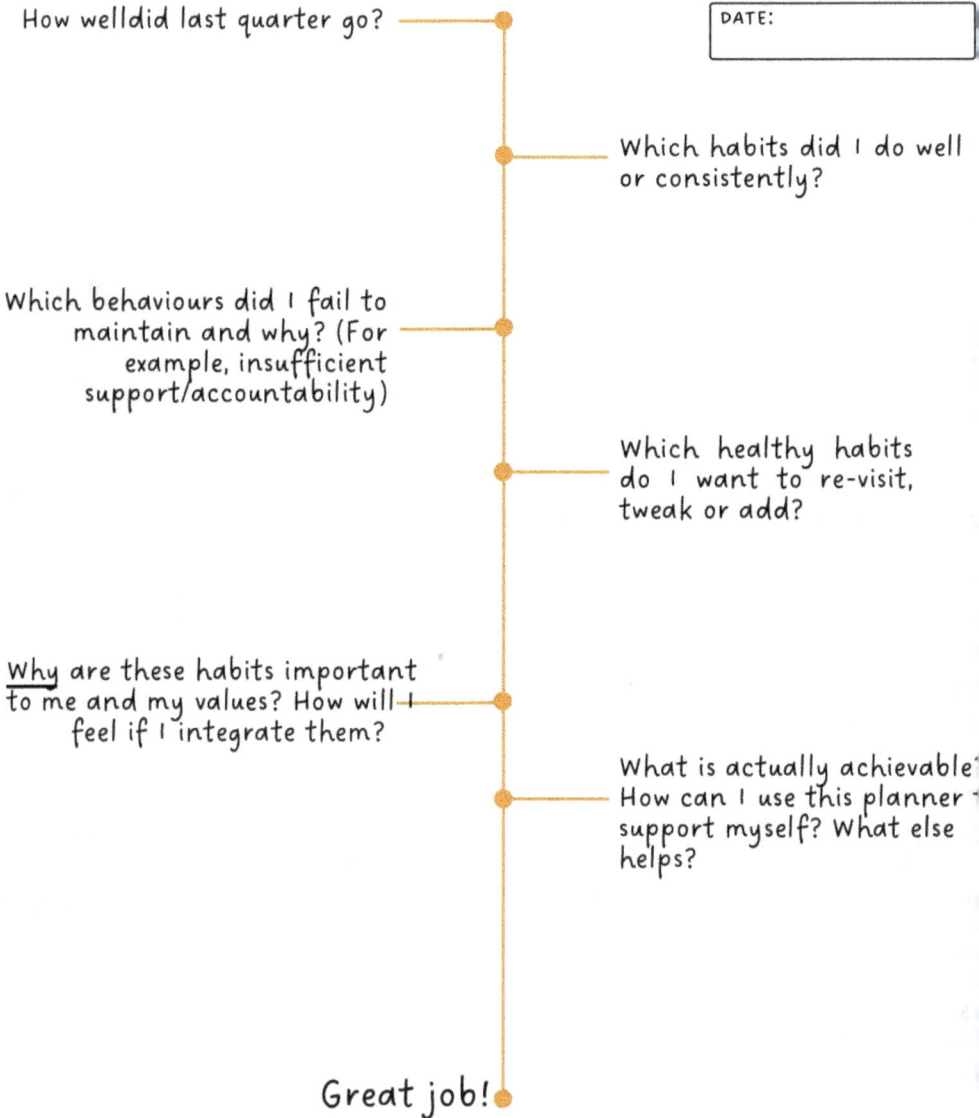

Habit goal-setting: Q 1

Journey layout ↘

Habit creation is about creating and cementing new neural pathways in the brain. If you're feeling jaded or fatigued by boxes & checklists, this variant 'journey layout' can be an effective way of disrupting your usual approach to habit goal-setting.

How welldid last quarter go?

DATE:

Which habits did I do well or consistently?

Which behaviours did I fail to maintain and why? (For example, insufficient support/accountability)

Which healthy habits do I want to re-visit, tweak or add?

Why are these habits important to me and my values? How will I feel if I integrate them?

What is actually achievable? How can I use this planner support myself? What else helps?

Great job!

NOW USE THE HABIT AND SELF CARE PAGES TO SUPPORT YOUR GOALS, AND REMEMB KIND TO YOURSELF! HABIT FORMING IS DIFFICULT FOR MOST PEOPLE, ADHD OR NO

42

Habit goal-setting: Q 2

The process of developing and solidifying new neural connections in the brain is known as habit formation. If you're tired with boxes and checklists, this variation 'journey layout' might be an excellent method to shake up your regular approach to habit goal-setting.

How did last quarter go?

DATE:

Which habits did I do well or consistently?

Which habits did I drop the ball on & why? (eg. not enough support/accountability)

Which healthy habits do I want to re-visit, tweak or add?

Why are these habits important to me and my values? How will I feel if I integrate them?

What is actually achievable? How can I use this planner to support myself? What else helps?

Great job!

NOW USE THE HABIT AND SELF CARE PAGES TO SUPPORT YOUR GOALS, AND REMEMBER TO KIND TO YOURSELF! HABIT FORMING IS DIFFICULT FOR MOST PEOPLE, ADHD OR NOT.

Habit goal-setting: Q 3

Habit creation is about creating and cementing new neural pathways in the brain. If you're feeling jaded or fatigued by boxes & checklists, this variant 'journey layout' can be an effective way of disrupting your usual approach to habit goal-setting.

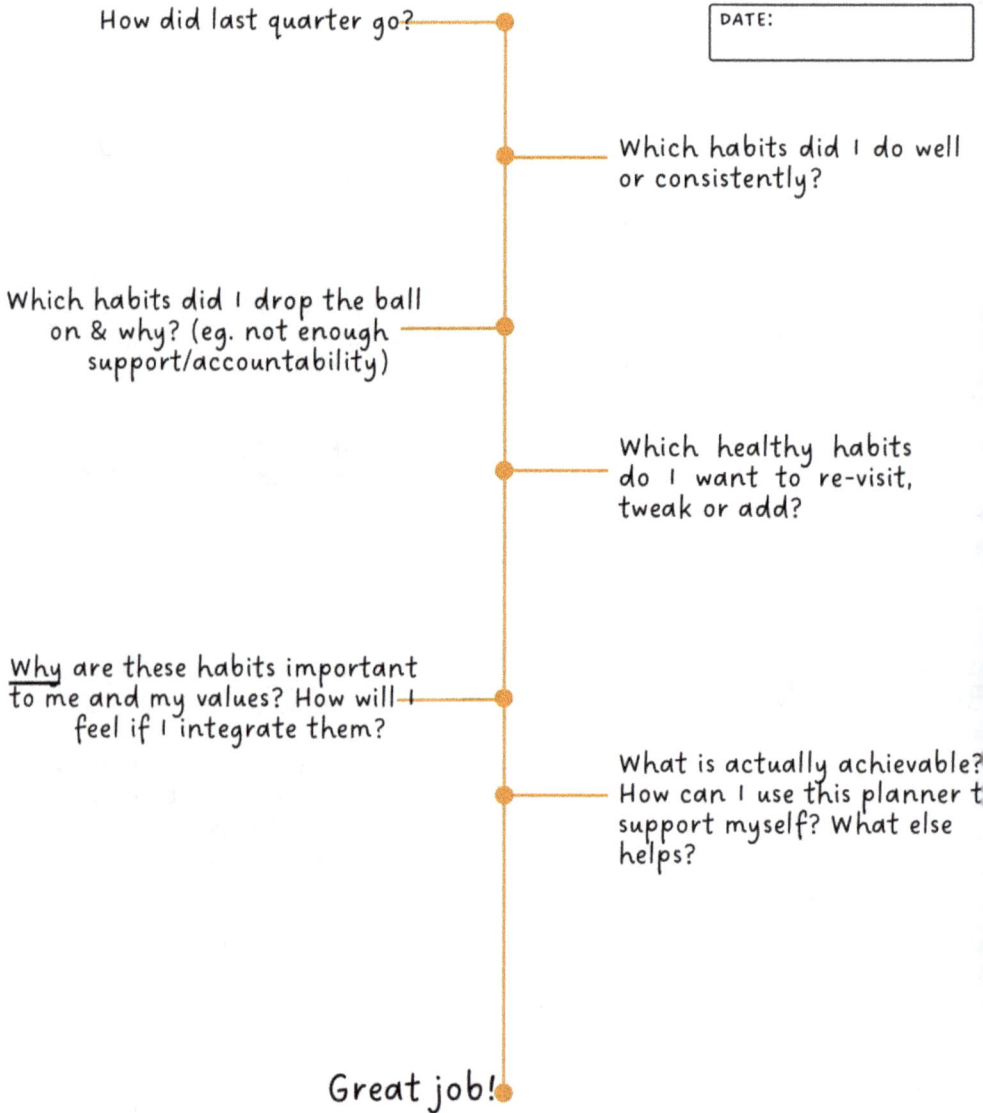

How did last quarter go?

DATE:

Which habits did I do well or consistently?

Which habits did I drop the ball on & why? (eg. not enough support/accountability)

Which healthy habits do I want to re-visit, tweak or add?

Why are these habits important to me and my values? How will I feel if I integrate them?

What is actually achievable? How can I use this planner t support myself? What else helps?

Great job!

NOW USE THE HABIT AND SELF CARE PAGES TO SUPPORT YOUR GOALS, AND REMEMB
KIND TO YOURSELF! HABIT FORMING IS DIFFICULT FOR MOST PEOPLE, ADHD OR NO

44

Habit goal-setting: Q 4

Habit creation is about creating and cementing new neural pathways in the brain. If you're feeling jaded or fatigued by boxes & checklists, this variant 'journey layout' can be an effective way of disrupting your usual approach to habit goal-setting.

How did last quarter go?

DATE:

Which habits did I do well or consistently?

Which habits did I drop the ball on & why? (eg. not enough support/accountability)

Which healthy habits do I want to re-visit, tweak or add?

Why are these habits important to me and my values? How will I feel if I integrate them?

What is actually achievable? How can I use this planner to support myself? What else helps?

Great job!

OW USE THE HABIT AND SELF CARE PAGES TO SUPPORT YOUR GOALS, AND REMEMBER TO IND TO YOURSELF! HABIT FORMING IS DIFFICULT FOR MOST PEOPLE, ADHD OR NOT.

45

Habit evaluation

Now you've created some goals and identified which habits will help you get there, choose one habit and get granular. Remember that you're not always starting from scratch - you may already be doing some things that support this habit, but a little tweaking and intention/motivation may help you break through & be more consistent!

MY GOAL OR NEW HABIT:

STOP DOING

DO
LESS OF

KEEP
DOIN
G

DO
MORE OF

START DOING

MOTIVATION OR INCENTIVE:

Limiting self-belief reframe

ADHDers, whether diagnosed early or late in life, carry a lot of negative inner narratives, limiting self-beliefs, and learned helplessness as a result of years of being misunderstood and not understanding how to get the most out of our uniquely-wired brains. This isn't going to be easy; be kind to yourself. If you're working with an ADHD coach (which I strongly suggest!), you may use this list to collaborate with them. The first stage is to identify the negative signals you got from your parents/caregivers/teachers, as well as your social milieu. The second stage is to reframe them in light of what science has to say about the ADHD brain and begin rewiring your neural networks.

	LIMITING SELF-BELIEF	REFRAME TO EMPOWER	REPEAT!
1			◯
2			◯
3			◯
4			◯
5			◯
6			◯
7			◯

Self-care

In this section:

tips & how
it works

Self-care

How to use:

☑ Now you've got some habit goals set, it's time to track your progress using the sleep, screen time, exercise and mood trackers. And there are meds trackers too (obvs).

☑ These trackers are a no-guilt, no-shame zone. Bandwagons can (and often must) be fallen off. Days will be missed. No one is perfect when it comes to executing a habit 365 days a year - the important thing is to pick it back up and keep going... keep it light and not so serious!

JUST IN CASE YOU'RE curious

The science bits
OUR PLANNER DESIGN

ADHD NEUROLOGICAL TRAIT	
WHEN IT COMES TO THE NATURAL TENDENCIES OF THE ADHD BRAIN, SELF-CARE IS A MAJOR AREA FOR IMPROVEMENT. WE'RE JUST DUMB AT IT.	WE NEED A LOT OF TANGIBLE SUPPORT WITH HABIT TRACKERS BECAUSE WHEN WE CAN SEE WHAT WE'RE ACHIEVING, WE FEEL LIKE WE'RE ON TOP OF THE WORLD, AND THAT DOPAMINE HIT FUELS CONSISTENCY.
DESIRE FOR HEALTHY HABITS, BUT FRUSTRATION LINKED TO LACK OF CONSISTENCY AROUND HABITS & DISCIPLINE	HABIT GOAL CHECKBOX REMINDERS ON MONTHLY, WEEKLY, AND DAILY PLANNING PAGE LEVELS (CONNECTED TO DISTINCT HABIT/GOAL PAGES)
LOWER LEVELS OF NATURALLY OCCURRING DOPAMINE AND NOREPINEPHRINE	COLOR CODING VISUAL TRACKERS, WHICH ARE A VISUAL DOPAMINE HIT

Mood tracker

A simple way to track your moods and emotions across the year. Use with the journal pages.

	J	F	M	A	M	J	J	A	S	O	N	D
1												
2												
3												
4												
5												
6												
7												
8												
9												
10												
11												
12												
13												
14												
15												
16												
17												
18												
19												
20												
21												
22												
23												
24												
25												
26												
27												
28												
29												
30												
31												

EMOTION KEY:

happy ☐
relaxed ☐
calm ☐
excitable ☐
focused ☐
high-energy ☐
annoyed ☐
frustrated ☐
angry ☐
tired ☐
anxious ☐
upset ☐
panicky ☐
miserable ☐
depressed ☐
not myself ☐
lonely ☐
overwhelmed ☐
☐
☐
☐
☐

Add your own emotions and colour coding here

Self-care routine

MORNING SELF-CARE

☐ _____
☐ _____
☐ _____
☐ _____
☐ _____
☐ _____
☐ _____
☐ _____

NIGHT SELF-CARE

☐ _____
☐ _____
☐ _____
☐ _____
☐ _____
☐ _____
☐ _____
☐ _____

Rate your self-care right now

1	2	3	4	5	6	7	8	9	10

N-EXISTENT   SOME DAYS   CONSISTENT

CHANGES TO MAKE SO I CAN BE MORE CONSISTENT:

Sleep tracker

Track your hours sleep per night each week. Scale is 1 to 10 hrs sleep.

BEDTIME ROUTINE

- [ ] _____
- [ ] _____
- [ ] _____
- [ ] _____

My sleep goal:

WEEKDAYS:

WEEKENDS:

	1	2	3	4	5	6	7	8	9	10
MON										
TUES										
WED										
THUR										
FRI										
SAT										
SUN										

	1	2	3	4	5	6	7	8	9	10
MON										
TUES										
WED										
THUR										
FRI										
SAT										
SUN										

Screen time tracker

Colour in each day to reflect how much screen time you had.

	J	F	M	A	M	J	J	A	S	O	N	D
1												
2												
3												
4												
5												
6												
7												
8												
9												
10												
11												
12												
13												
14												
15												
16												
17												
18												
19												
20												
21												
22												
23												
24												
25												
26												
27												
28												
29												
30												
31												
32												

My screen time goal:

WEEKDAYS:

WEEKENDS:

COLOUR KEY:

zero

< 30 min

1-2 hrs

3-4 hrs

5-6 hrs

7-8 hrs

9-10 hrs

> 10 hrs

Tracker:

Blank tracker for habits or symptoms (add your own heading)

	J	F	M	A	M	J	J	A	S	O	N	D
1												
2												
3												
4												
5												
6												
7												
8												
9												
10												
11												
12												
13												
14												
15												
16												
17												
18												
19												
20												
21												
22												
23												
24												
25												
26												
27												
28												
29												
30												
31												

DETAILS:

KEY:

ADHD + exercise

Exercise has been shown to be so powerful in reducing the adverse symptoms of ADHD, that doctors actually prescribe it as a supplemental treatment for patients managing their symptoms with medication, therapy and/or nutrition.

Why is it so effective?

Exercise helps reduce the 'scattered brain' typical of ADHD by increasing the neurotransmitters dopamine and norepinephrine - both of which are key in regulating the attention system. ADHD brains produce less dopamine and norepinephrine than neurotypical brains, so the difference when you exercise is noticeable.

People with ADHD typically have higher levels of energy or hyperactivity than the ordinary person, and exercise is a natural release for this pent up energy. If you are sedentary, your mind will find ways to use up that excess energy, leading to a more hyperactive and racing mind.

Exercise also creates the ideal environment for your brain to grow new neurons, connectors and positive pathways. This environment occurs when intense exercise triggers the release of a chemical called brain-derived neurotropic factor (BDNF).

Cool, hey? So if you're not medicated/on a wait-list for diagnosis or just feeling meh, try adding more intense exercise into your schedule and see if it helps. Even a decent dance session in your living room gets your heart rate up and those happy dopamine hormones flowing! :)

Fitness tracker

Use this 4-week fitness tracker to track any fitness you engage in, be it planned, incidental, intense or casual. Undated so you don't feel like a failure if you miss a day or week. Fill it out as you need, re-print as needed!

GET THAT DOPA HIT!

WEEK OF: _____   M   T   W   T   F   S   S

-    O O O O O O O
-    O O O O O O O
-    O O O O O O O
-    O O O O O O O
-    O O O O O O O

WEEK OF: _____   M   T   W   T   F   S   S

-    O O O O O O O
-    O O O O O O O
-    O O O O O O O
-    O O O O O O O
-    O O O O O O O

WEEK OF: _____   M   T   W   T   F   S   S

-    O O O O O O O
-    O O O O O O O
-    O O O O O O O
-    O O O O O O O
-    O O O O O O O

WEEK OF: _____   M   T   W   T   F   S   S

-    O O O O O O O
-    O O O O O O O
-    O O O O O O O
-    O O O O O O O
-    O O O O O O O

Notes from therapy

THERAPIST:

MON   TUE   WED   THU   FRI   SAT   SUN

○   ○   ○   ○   ○   ○   ○

DATE:

_____

_____

_____

_____

_____

_____

_____

_____

_____

_____

_____

_____

_____

_____

_____

_____

_____

_____

_____

_____

_____

_____

_____

_____

_____

Notes to take to therapy

THERAPIST:

MON	TUE	WED	THU	FRI	SAT	SUN
○	○	○	○	○	○	○

DATE:

_____

_____

_____

_____

_____

_____

_____

_____

_____

_____

_____

_____

_____

_____

_____

_____

_____

_____

_____

_____

_____

_____

_____

ADHD coaching
SESSION NOTES

COACH: ______________________

MON ○ TUE ○ WED ○ THU ○ FRI ○ SAT ○ SUN ○

DATE:

Medical appointments

DATE: / / DOCTOR:

TO DISCUSS:

- [ ] _____
- [ ] _____
- [ ] _____
- [ ] _____
- [ ] _____

NOTES:

PRESCRIPTION? Y N [ ] [ ]

DATE: / / DOCTOR:

TO DISCUSS:

- [ ] _____
- [ ] _____
- [ ] _____
- [ ] _____
- [ ] _____

NOTES:

PRESCRIPTION? Y N [ ] [ ]

DATE: / / DOCTOR:

TO DISCUSS:

- [ ] _____
- [ ] _____
- [ ] _____
- [ ] _____
- [ ] _____

NOTES:

PRESCRIPTION? Y N [ ] [ ]

Quarterly medication tracker

MEDICINE:DOSE:

FREQUENCY:

JANUARY

M T W T F S S

How did I feel?

Refill?

FEBRUARY

M T W T F S S

How did I feel?

Refill?

MARCH

M T W T F S S

How did I feel?

Refill?

Quarterly
~~medication~~ tracker

MEDICINE:DOSE:

FREQUENCY:

APRIL

		M	T	W	T	F	S	S
How did I feel?		○	○	○	○	○	○	○
---		○	○	○	○	○	○	○
---		○	○	○	○	○	○	○
---		○	○	○	○	○	○	○
----------------------------	*Refill?* ☐	○	○	○	○	○	○	○

MAY

		M	T	W	T	F	S	S
How did I feel?		○	○	○	○	○	○	○
---		○	○	○	○	○	○	○
---		○	○	○	○	○	○	○
---		○	○	○	○	○	○	○
----------------------------	*Refill?* ☐	○	○	○	○	○	○	○

JUNE

		M	T	W	T	F	S	S
How did I feel?		○	○	○	○	○	○	○
---		○	○	○	○	○	○	○
---		○	○	○	○	○	○	○
---		○	○	○	○	○	○	○
----------------------------	*Refill?* ☐	○	○	○	○	○	○	○

Quarterly medication tracker

EDICINE:DOSE:		FREQUENCY:

JULY

	M	T	W	T	F	S	S
How did I feel?	○	○	○	○	○	○	○
------------------------------	○	○	○	○	○	○	○
------------------------------	○	○	○	○	○	○	○
------------------------------	○	○	○	○	○	○	○
------------------ Refill? ☐	○	○	○	○	○	○	○

AUGUST

	M	T	W	T	F	S	S
How did I feel?	○	○	○	○	○	○	○
------------------------------	○	○	○	○	○	○	○
------------------------------	○	○	○	○	○	○	○
------------------------------	○	○	○	○	○	○	○
------------------ Refill? ☐	○	○	○	○	○	○	○

SEPTEMBER

	M	T	W	T	F	S	S
How did I feel?	○	○	○	○	○	○	○
------------------------------	○	○	○	○	○	○	○
------------------------------	○	○	○	○	○	○	○
------------------------------	○	○	○	○	○	○	○
------------------ Refill? ☐	○	○	○	○	○	○	○

Quarterly medication tracker

MEDICINE:DOSE:		FREQUENCY:

OCTOBER

M T W T F S S

How did I feel?

-------------------------------- Refill? ☐

NOVEMBER

M T W T F S S

How did I feel?

-------------------------------- Refill? ☐

DECEMBER

M T W T F S S

How did I feel?

-------------------------------- Refill? ☐

Multiple medication tracker

	M	T	W	T	F	S	S
Medicine: Dose: Freq:	○	○	○	○	○	○	○
Medicine: Dose: Freq: Medicine: Dose: Freq:	○	○	○	○	○	○	○
Medicine: Dose: Freq:	○	○	○	○	○	○	○
	○	○	○	○	○	○	○

Refill? ☐

	M	T	W	T	F	S	S
Medicine: Dose: Freq:	○	○	○	○	○	○	○
Medicine: Dose: Freq: Medicine: Dose: Freq:	○	○	○	○	○	○	○
Medicine: Dose: Freq:	○	○	○	○	○	○	○
	○	○	○	○	○	○	○

Refill? ☐

	M	T	W	T	F	S	S
Medicine: Dose: Freq:	○	○	○	○	○	○	○
Medicine: Dose: Freq: Medicine: Dose: Freq:	○	○	○	○	○	○	○
Medicine: Dose: Freq:	○	○	○	○	○	○	○
	○	○	○	○	○	○	○

Refill? ☐

5

In this section:

Digital de-clutter

Home de-clutter

Plant health tracker

Meal planner

Family meal planner

Grocery list (with clear category sections)

tips & how it works

Domestic Domination

How to use:

Out of sight, out of mind no more! Use these pre-filled lists to organise a regular cleaning & maintenance routine, both in the home and in your digital space.

Our templates include meal planning, grocery lists, a plant health tracker and pre-filled de-cluttering lists, as well as blank spaces to add your own items. Print each page as many times as you need, and use as often or infrequently as you need! #norules #adhdyourway

ADHD NEUROLOGICAL TRAIT

The science bits
OUR PLANNER DESIGN

BOREDOM AND CHUNKING TASKS DOWN ARE TWO THINGS ADHD BRAINS STRUGGLE WITH, SO MUNDANE TASKS WITH MANY STEPS ARE ALMOST GUARANTEED TO BE AVOIDED AT ALL COSTS

WE'VE PRE-FILLED THE DE-CLUTTER LISTS WITH TASKS SO YOU DON'T HAVE TO COME UP WITH THEM YOURSELF. USE REGULAR REWARDS TO MOTIVATE YOU, OR TRY BODY DOUBLING (DE-CLUTTERING WITH A FRIEND)

DUE TO OUR DESIRE FOR NOVELTY, MEAL-PREPPING CAN FEEL BORING OR THE MANY STEPS INVOLVED ARE TAXING, SO WE AVOID IT AND GO FOR LESS-NUTRITIOUS OPTIONS

OUR MEAL-PLANNERS INCLUDE REMINDERS TO TRY NEW MEALS, SO YOU'RE MORE LIKELY TO BE MOTIVATED TO COOK

HYPER-FOCUS ALSO MEANS WE DON'T NOTICE WHEN OUR PLANTS ARE DYING

PRINT OUR PLANT HEALTH TRACKER & PUT IT ON YOUR MIRROR SO YOU REMEMBER

Digital de-clutter

We are taught to clean our homes, but our devices need some TLC too! Some clean-up tasks don't need to be done every month, but de-cluttering regularly makes the task less daunting. Find a routine that works for you & your brain!

MONTHLY CLEAN-UPS	1	2	3	4	5	6	7	8	9	10	11	12
Email inbox												
Delete spam emails	○	○	○	○	○	○	○	○	○	○	○	○
Archive old emails	○	○	○	○	○	○	○	○	○	○	○	○
Delete emails with large attachments	○	○	○	○	○	○	○	○	○	○	○	○
Unsubscribe (use free tool like Unroll.me)	○	○	○	○	○	○	○	○	○	○	○	○
○	○	○	○	○	○	○	○	○	○	○	○	○
Smartphone												
Back-up photos/videos to cloud storage	○	○	○	○	○	○	○	○	○	○	○	○
Delete photos from device	○	○	○	○	○	○	○	○	○	○	○	○
Delete downloaded podcast episodes	○	○	○	○	○	○	○	○	○	○	○	○
Turn off auto-download for podcast	○	○	○	○	○	○	○	○	○	○	○	○
subs Wipe down with 70% isopropyl	○	○	○	○	○	○	○	○	○	○	○	○
wipes	○	○	○	○	○	○	○	○	○	○	○	○
Computer/laptop												
Trash old files/folders	○	○	○	○	○	○	○	○	○	○	○	○
Run system updates & update antivirus	○	○	○	○	○	○	○	○	○	○	○	○
software Delete duplicate files	○	○	○	○	○	○	○	○	○	○	○	○
Delete files in downloads folder	○	○	○	○	○	○	○	○	○	○	○	○
Take app inventory & uninstall old & unused	○	○	○	○	○	○	○	○	○	○	○	○
Invent a file naming system & stick to it	○	○	○	○	○	○	○	○	○	○	○	○
Clean up your desktop folders*	○	○	○	○	○	○	○	○	○	○	○	○
Empty trash	○	○	○	○	○	○	○	○	○	○	○	○
Wipe down with 70% isopropyl wipes	○	○	○	○	○	○	○	○	○	○	○	○
○	○	○	○	○	○	○	○	○	○	○	○	○
Tablet												
Back-up photos/videos to cloud storage	○	○	○	○	○	○	○	○	○	○	○	○
Delete photos from device	○	○	○	○	○	○	○	○	○	○	○	○
Delete downloaded podcast episodes	○	○	○	○	○	○	○	○	○	○	○	○
Turn off auto-download for podcast subs	○	○	○	○	○	○	○	○	○	○	○	○
Trash old files/folders	○	○	○	○	○	○	○	○	○	○	○	○
Run system updates & update antivirus software	○	○	○	○	○	○	○	○	○	○	○	○
Take app inventory & uninstall old & unused	○	○	○	○	○	○	○	○	○	○	○	○
Empty trash	○	○	○	○	○	○	○	○	○	○	○	○
Wipe down with 70% isopropyl wipes	○	○	○	○	○	○	○	○	○	○	○	○
○	○	○	○	○	○	○	○	○	○	○	○	○
Social												
Archive old messages on WhatsApp, FB	○	○	○	○	○	○	○	○	○	○	○	○
etc. Delete old text messages	○	○	○	○	○	○	○	○	○	○	○	○
Delete old voicemails	○	○	○	○	○	○	○	○	○	○	○	○
○	○	○	○	○	○	○	○	○	○	○	○	○
○	○	○	○	○	○	○	○	○	○	○	○	○
○	○	○	○	○	○	○	○	○	○	○	○	○

Home de-clutter

SPRING	SUMME
AUTUM	R
N	WINTER

Tip: try 'body doubling' to get big tasks like this done. De-clutter with a friend, and then help them in return.

LIVING SPACE

- ◯ Books
- ◯ Burnt candles
- ◯ Knick knacks
- ◯ Old   birthday
- ◯ cards Toys
- ◯ Art/sculpture
- ◯ Old throw rugs
- ◯ Stained cushions
- ◯
- ◯

BEDROOM

- ◯ Unused/old clothes
- ◯ Seasonal clothes
- ◯ Cables & cords
- ◯ Knick knacks
- ◯ Journals
- ◯ Books
- ◯ Under bed storage
- ◯ Accessories/bags/hats
- ◯ Unused shoes
- ◯ Jewellery/perfume

KID'S BEDROOM

- ◯ Books
- ◯ Toys
- ◯ Knick knacks
- ◯ Old birthday cards
- ◯ Outgrown clothes
- ◯ Outdoor Games
- ◯ Art & craft
- ◯ School projects
- ◯ Handmade art on walls
- ◯

BATHROOMS

- ◯ Appliances/cords
- ◯ Burnt candles
- ◯ Soap containers
- ◯ Shampoo/conditioner
- ◯ Bath toys
- ◯ Toilet roll refresh
- ◯ Old cosmetics
- ◯ Old toiletries
- ◯ Expired medicine
- ◯ Expired suncream

KITCHEN

- ◯ Expired pantry items
- ◯ Expired fridge items
- ◯ Old freezer/deep freeze
- ◯ Worn cleaning clothes
- ◯ Worn dish towels
- ◯ Broken glasses/crockery
- ◯ Tupperware missing lids
- ◯ Broken serving dishes
- ◯ Broken/unused appliance
- ◯

LAUNDRY

- ◯ Under laundry sink
- ◯ Expired cleaning products
- ◯ Toilet paper refresh
- ◯ Odd sock sort
- ◯ Storage de-clutter
- ◯ Mouldy wet-weather gear
- ◯ Vacuum cleaner
- ◯ Clean cycle washing
- ◯ mach.
- ◯

GARAGE

- ◯ Bikes
- ◯ Skateboards
- ◯ Old tools
- ◯ Boxes of old stuff
- ◯ Cleaning products
- ◯ Old paint tins
- ◯ Fuel cans
- ◯ Car cleaning equipment
- ◯
- ◯

OFFICE

- ◯ Old pens/stationary
- ◯ Cameras, technology
- ◯ Cords & chargers
- ◯ Receipts
- ◯ Paperwork
- ◯ Unused notepads sort
- ◯ Unused craft items
- ◯ Business/self-help books
- ◯ Print ink
- ◯ Old batteries

OUTDOORS

- ◯ Mower
- ◯ Gardening tools
- ◯ Hose
- ◯ Old pot plants
- ◯ Pet gear
- ◯ Trampoline
- ◯ Play equipment
- ◯ Outdoor furniture
- ◯ Hammock
- ◯ Camping/trekking gear

Home de-clutter

Plant health tracker

If you're anything like me, your one-track ADHD brain often gets so hyper-focused you forget to water your leafy friends. Print this page & put it somewhere you'll see it everyday (like your mirror) so you don't forget to water & care for your plants.

PLANT FRIEND: NOTES: M T W T F S S

LIKES SUN: Y /

N NEEDS WATER:

PLANT FRIEND: NOTES: M T W T F S S

LIKES SUN: Y /

N NEEDS WATER:

PLANT FRIEND: NOTES: M T W T F S S

LIKES SUN: Y /

N NEEDS WATER:

PLANT FRIEND: NOTES: M T W T F S S

LIKES SUN: Y /

N NEEDS WATER:

PLANT FRIEND: NOTES: M T W T F S S

LIKES SUN: Y /

N NEEDS WATER:

Pet feeding tracker

MONTH:

Unless your furry friend has magically evolved to have opposable thumbs and can open the cupboard and feed itself, you're gonna need this template. ;)

FURRY FRIEND: NOTES: M   T   W   T   F   S   S
_____
_____
_____
_____

FURRY FRIEND: NOTES: M   T   W   T   F   S   S
_____
_____
_____
_____

FURRY FRIEND: NOTES: M   T   W   T   F   S   S
_____
_____
_____
_____

FURRY FRIEND: NOTES: M   T   W   T   F   S   S
_____
_____
_____
_____

FURRY FRIEND: NOTES: M   T   W   T   F   S   S
_____
_____
_____
_____

Meal planner

Tip! Novelty = motivation, so add a <u>new recipe</u> you haven't <u>made before</u>

MONDAY

TUESDAY

WEDNESDAY

THURSDAY

FRIDAY

SATURDAY

SUNDAY

BREAKFAST OPTIONS (ROTATE):

☐ _____
☐ _____
☐ _____
☐ _____

LUNCH OPTIONS (ROTATE):

☐ _____
☐ _____
☐ _____
☐ _____
☐ _____

SNACKS + CRAVINGS:

_____
☐ _____
☐ _____
☐ _____
☐ _____
☐ _____

NEED MOTIVATION TO EAT WELL? DO A HABIT VISUALISATION JOURNAL PAGE

73

Family meal planner

MONDAY

☐

TUESDAY

☐

WEDNESDAY

☐

THURSDAY

☐

FRIDAY

☐

SATURDAY

☐

SUNDAY

☐

BREAKFAST OPTIONS (ROTATE):

☐ _____

☐ _____

☐ _____

☐ _____

LUNCH OPTIONS (ROTATE):

☐ _____

☐ _____

☐ _____

☐ _____

☐ _____

BABY/TODDLER FOOD:

☐ _____

☐ _____

☐ _____

SNACKS + CRAVINGS:

☐ _____

☐ _____

☐ _____

Grocery list

VEGGIES & FRUITS

DAIRY

FROZEN

PANTRY

PROTEIN

BAKERY

HYGIENE & MEDICAL

CLEANING

OTHER

DRINKS

BAGS

COOL BAG

REWARDS CARD

GOT 'EM!

6

In this section:

Phone Call Focus Flowers x 6

The Hyper-focus Lotus

Productivity Power Petals

tips & how it works

Focus flowers

How to use:

☑ I've developed three powerful tools to help you manage hyper-focus challenges in everyday life and work life.

☑ The Phone Call Focus Flowers help your mind focus (when it would usually wander) when you're talking to your parents, sister, friend etc on the phone. The Hyper-Focus Lotus and Productivity Power Petals are both tools to use as self-care prompts when you're deep in hyper-focus work / study mode.

JUST IN CASE YOU'RE curious

The science bits

ADHD NEUROLOGICAL TRAIT	OUR PLANNER DESIGN
OUR MINDS TEND TO WANDER AS DIVERGENT THOUGHTS RACE THROUGH AT A 100 MILES A SECOND, AND WE CAN SPACE OUT WHEN SOMEONE IS TALKING TO US AND WE'RE BORED	WE KNOW YOU WANT TO LISTEN WHEN YOUR FRIEND IS VENTING ABOUT HER TERRIBLE BOSS, SO USE THE 'PHONE CALL FOCUS FLOWER' TO ENGAGE YOUR BRAIN WHILE YOU CHAT ON THE PHONE
WHEN WE HYPER-FOCUS WE BECOME SO IMMERSED THAT WE FORGET TO EAT, DRINK AND MOVE, SOMETIMES FOR 6 HOURS OR MORE.	PUT OUR SIGNATURE 'HYPER-FOCUS LOTUS FLOWER' OR 'PRODUCTIVITY POWER PETALS' NEXT TO YOU WHILE YOU'RE DEEP DIVING INTO HYPER-FQCUS, TO MAKE SURE YOU REMEMBER TO TAKE BREAKS AND LOOK AFTER YOURSELF. COLOUR IN A PETAL EVERY TIME YOU COMPLETE A MINI BREAK.

Why do our thoughts wander?

Our ADHD brains drift during conversations because we have an internal motor that is constantly whirring, and stimulants in our environment, mind or the conversation itself can catch our curiosity and we chase it down a rabbit hole. We appear dreamy or vacant, when actually we are very present with our own thoughts and ponderings.

Dr. Edward Hallowell speaks beautifully of this in his recent book 'ADHD 2.0' (a must-read since Dr Hallowell himself has ADHD and has studied it for several decades). He says:

"Even when we're awake, we're dreaming, always creating, always searching... our imagination fuels our curiosity to find out what the noise was, or what was under the rock, or why the petri dish looks different from when we left it. If we weren't so dreamy and curious we could stay on track and never get distracted... We don't suffer from a 'deficit' of attention. Just the opposite. We've got an overabundance of attention, more attention than we can cope with; our constant challenge is to control it."

If we really want to still our wandering mind so we can focus on an important conversation or podcast, we can engage that drifting focus in a simple physical/mental task like colouring. I've found colouring makes it a lot easier to transfer or 'piggyback' that focus onto what the other person is saying and stay mentally present with them. It's essentially multitasking the ADHD way, and it helps us focus more!

Phone call focus flower #1

Phone call focus flower #2

Phone call focus flower #3

Phone call focus flower #5

Phone call focus flower #6

Hyperfocus + ADHD

Our ADHD brain enjoys hyper-focusing on tasks that it finds intriguing. It's one of our special abilities! We are extremely excited and 'locked in' when we are in a state of hyper-focus. Because excitement is the ADHD brain's first concern, everyday actions such as eating, drinking water, or going to the restroom become inconsequential - nearly invisible!!

So why do the Hyper-Focus Lotus and Productive Power Petals work so well?

They're designed to compete to be equally (or as close as possible to equally) motivating as the hyper-focus task. Because our ADHD brains prioritise dopamine/fun/novelty in a task, gamifying mundane tasks is a way to make sure they get done. We like the reward/challenge of completing the lotus/flower colouring alongside whatever is taking our focus.

Bonus tip: invest some $$$ and buy a fun/fancy water bottle that also motivates you to drink water.

The lotus with hyperfocus

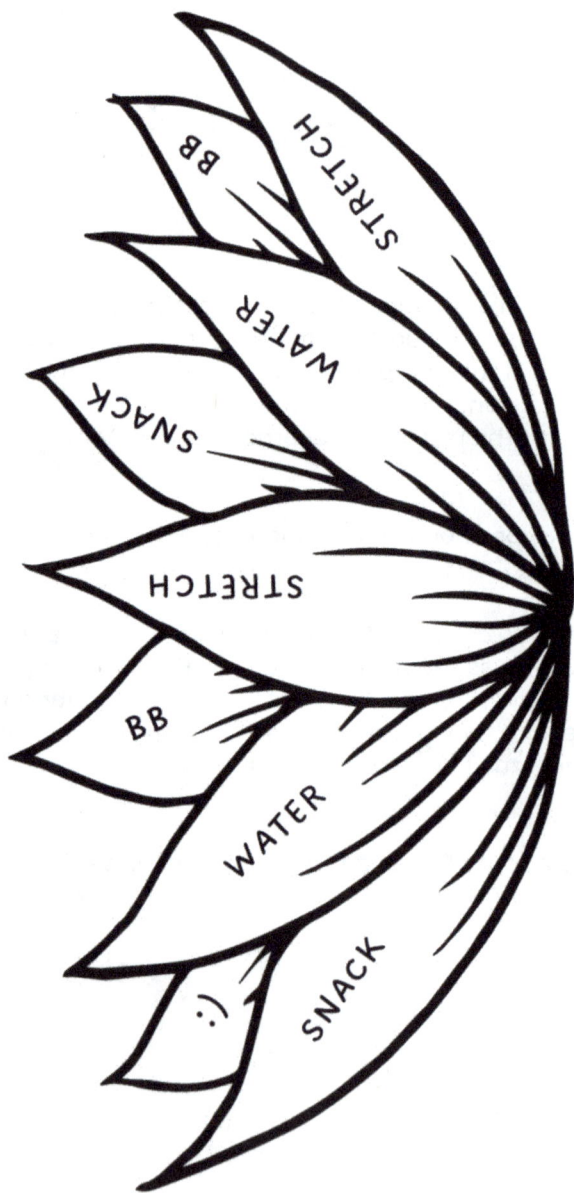

Put this lotus blossom next to you while you're deep in hyper-focus to remind you to take pauses and care for yourself. Every time you finish a brief break, colour in a flower.

Petal labels: STRETCH, BB, WATER, SNACK, STRETCH, BB, WATER, SNACK

Productivity power petals

Put this lotus flower next to you while you're deep diving into hyper-focus, to make sure you remember to take breaks and look after yourself. Colour in a petal every time you complete a mini break.

BB = bathroom break

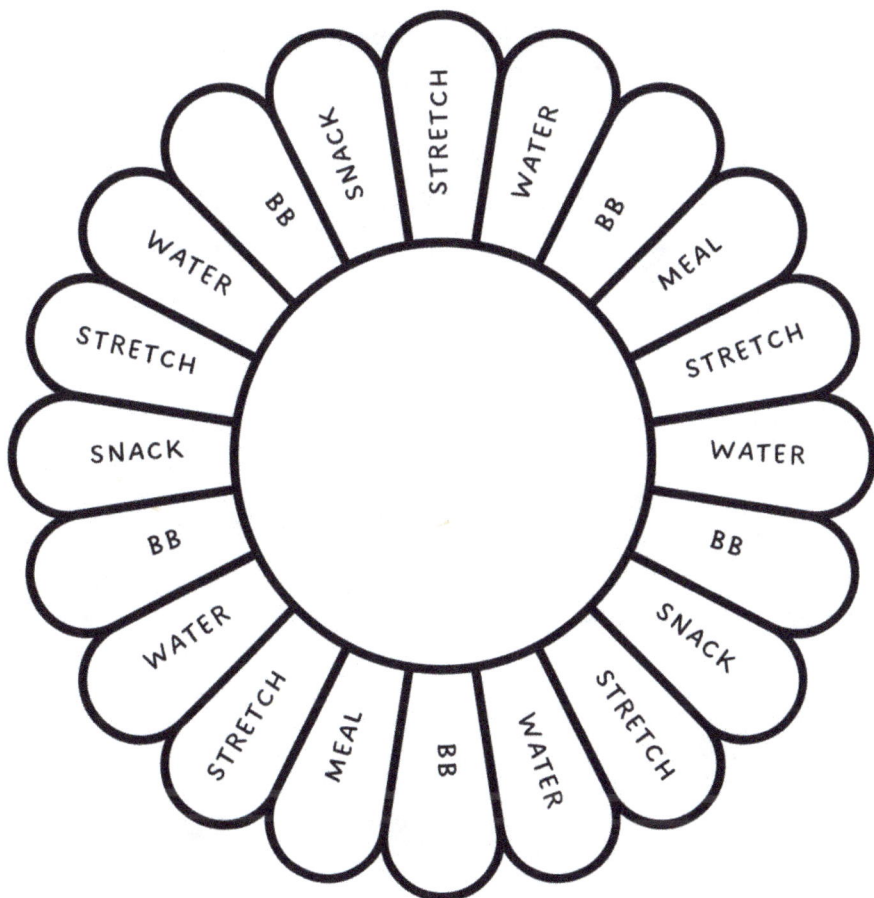

7

In this section:

tips & how
it works

Unwind
un-mind

How to use:

In this section, you'll find unique, offbeat tools I've created myself in an effort to disrupt my own self-defeating thought patterns and calm my hyperactive brain. They look deceptively simple, but they work because they ~~trick the mind into~~ finding more convergent strategies and getting out of the rut of divergent thinking we can find ourselves visiting often (see the Divergent thinking science page for more info).

Don't know where to start? Print out the 'Don't think, just do', 'Colour to Calm' or 'Symmetry Stress-Relief' pages and have them in easily accessible locations for when overwhelm and intense emotion hits.

The science bits

OUR PLANNER DESIGN

ADHD NEUROLOGICAL TRAIT

ADHD BRAINS ARE PRONE TO AN OVER-EMPHASIS ON DIVERGENT THINKING OVER CONVERGENT THINKING. IT'S EXHAUSTING FOR US WHEN WE LIVE IN THE HIGHLY STIMULATING DIVERGENT THINKING HEADSPACE ALL DAY, EVERY DAY

THIS SECTION AIMS TO BRING BALANCE. IF YOU WANT TO SLOW THE 'PINGING' IDEAS, TRY THE SYMMETRY TRACING EXERCISES 'SYMMETRY STRESS-RELIEF' TO ACTIVATE YOUR CONVERGENT THINKING BRAIN, AND FLEX THAT MUSCLE

WHEN OUR BRAINS ARE OVERWHELMED BY DIVERGENT THINKING AND ARE PRESENTED WITH OPEN-ENDED CHOICES, WE MOVE TO OUR AMYGDALA FREEZE RESPONSE AND SHUT DOWN

OUR 'DON'T THINK JUST DO' & 'COLOUR TO CALM' WORKSHEETS INCLUDE MODIFICATIONS FOR THE ADHD BRAIN SO THE DECISION IS TAKEN OFF YOUR PLATE AND YOU CAN TAKE FAST ACTION INSTEAD OF WALLOWING IN INDECISION & FAILURE

Don't think, just do

Feeling frazzled? I've got you! Often, we just need to calm our over-stimulated ADHD nervous system before we can make the next decision or next move. Self-care is a matter of priority - like putting fuel in your car. My tip? Don't overthink, just pick one thing from this cheat sheet and DO IT RIGHT NOW!! :) If you can't decide, pick number #2.

01	TRY A COLOURING/DRAWING EXERCISE IN OUR UNWIND UN-MIND SECTION	☐
02	MAKE YOURSELF A CUP OF TEA (OR YOUR FAVE HOT BEVERAGE - PLAIN HOT WATER IS GREAT TOO!). THE WARM LIQUID HELPS GROUND YOU IN YOUR BODY.	☐
03	HIDE FROM THE WORLD - TAKE A LONG SHOWER AND BURN A CANDLE TO CREATE A RETREAT/SPA VIBE	☐
04	GET MOVING AND RE-FOCUS YOUR MIND... PODCAST, EARPHONES AND A BRISK WALK	☐
05	TRY EFT TAPPING - IT REALLY HELPS! OR CLOSE YOUR EYES AND BALANCE ON ONE LEG - THIS HELPS TONE THE CEREBELLUM IN YOUR BRAIN.	☐
06	BRAIN DUMP - USE OUR TEMPLATES TO WRITE, OR RECORD YOURSELF INTO THE VOICE NOTES APP ON YOUR PHONE. YOU CAN DELETE LATER IF YOU WANT.	☐
07	DANCE PARTY (I HAVE A PLAYLIST CALLED 'ADHDANCE' ESPECIALLY FOR MOMENTS WHERE I NEED TO DANCE OUT MY NERVOUS/FRUSTRATED ENERGY)	☐
08	MINDFUL EATING - TRY TO EAT SOMETHING REALLY SLOWLY, CLOSE YOUR EYES AND NARROW YOUR FOCUS ON THE SENSATIONS, SMELLS, FLAVOURS AND SOUNDS.	☐

When I feel anxious...

List the calming strategies that have worked in the past - print this out and stick somewhere you'll see it.

01 ☐

02 ☐

03 ☐

04 ☐

05 ☐

06 ☐

07 ☐

08 ☐

Wind-down strategies

Because our ADHD brain can be a tad forgetful sometimes, we'll discover an awesome new hack or strategy that our brain loves, do it a million times in a week and then get so over it, we'll drop it and forget about it. The information seems to fall right out of our brain, because the next obsession is so immersive that it consumes our working memory. Before this happens, note your current obsession - fave music playlists, apps, stretching/yoga exercises and go-to meditations so you can find them again.

MEDITATIONS | STRETCHING/YOGA EXERCISES

APPS | MUSIC PLAYLISTS

Ever heard of binaural be
They've been shown to
really effective for ADH

Fave playlists for...

All in one space, for when you need one to match your mood or activity.

CLEANING:

HYPERFOCUS/WORK:

COMMUTE:

CHILLING:

EXERCISE:

COOKING:

Fave playlists

Add your own categories! ↰

All in one space, find easily to match your mood or activity.

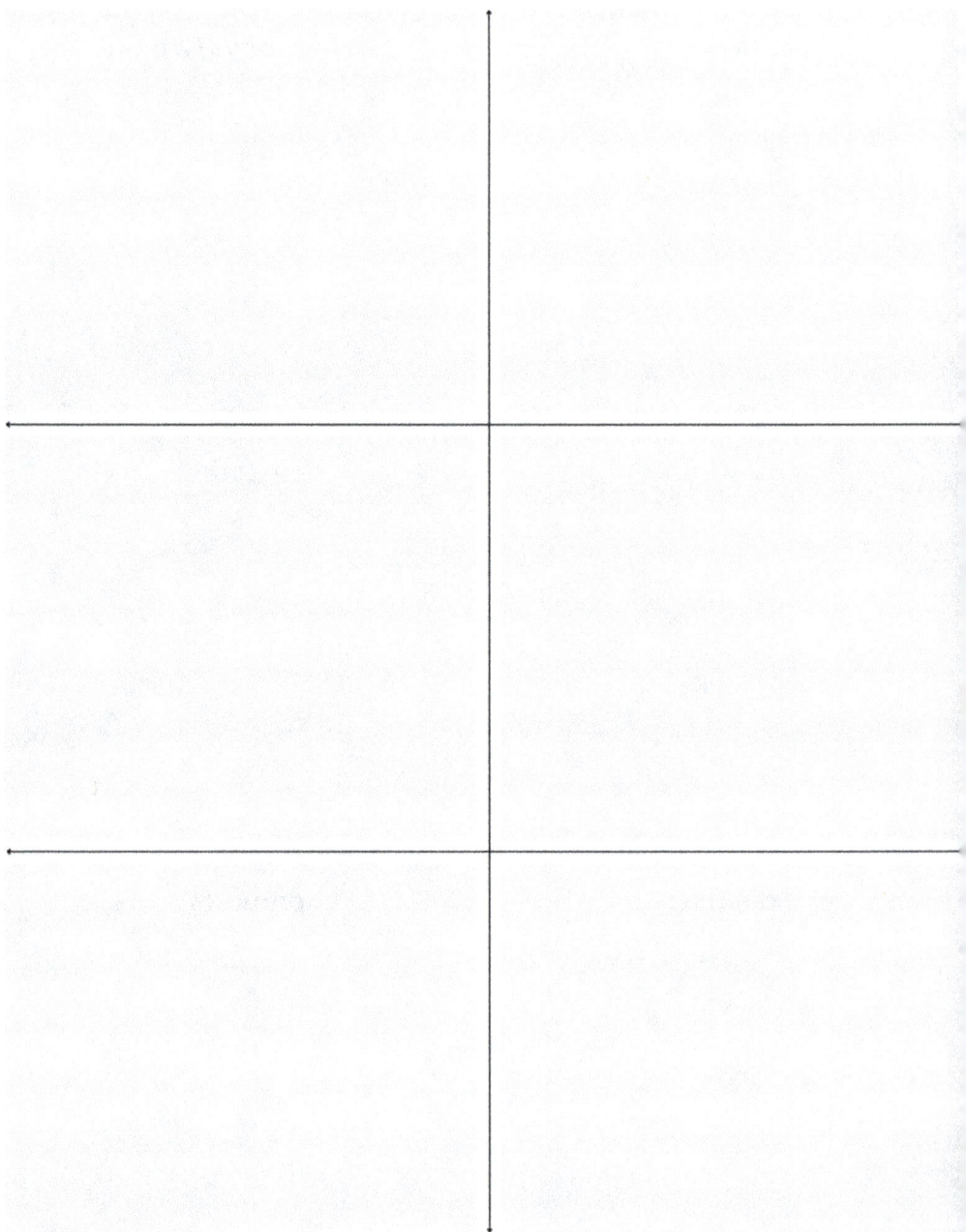

Colour to calm

One way to calm the hyperactive or over-stimulated ADHD brain is to give it fewer choices and more boundaries. Colouring in is an effective way to take the chaos of thoughts and direct them between the lines - even if just to give you temporary relief and a sense of peace.

To reduce overwhelm and barriers, each page includes directions on which colour & shades to use. One less decision to make! I've included multiple geometric designs ranging from simple to more complex. **See what your mind is drawn to in the moment.**

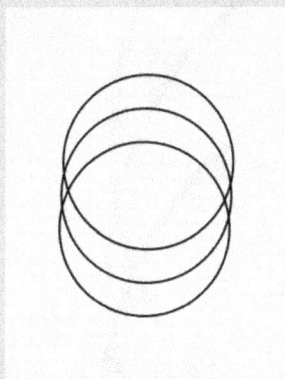

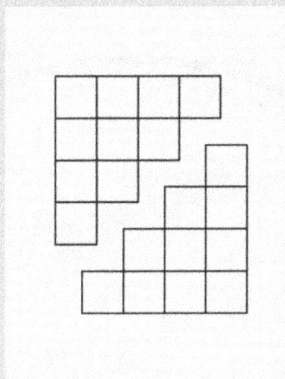

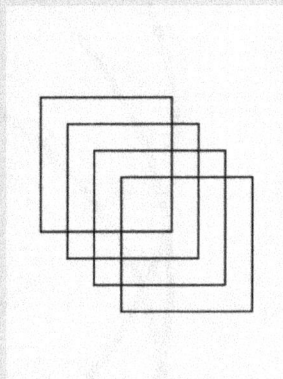

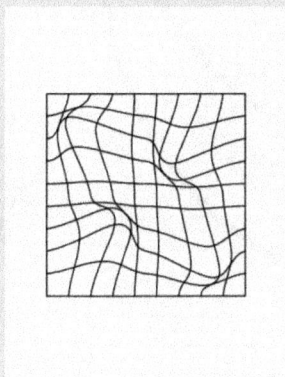

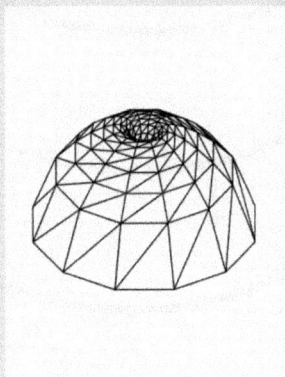

Colour in this line drawing
only using <u>shades of yellow.</u>

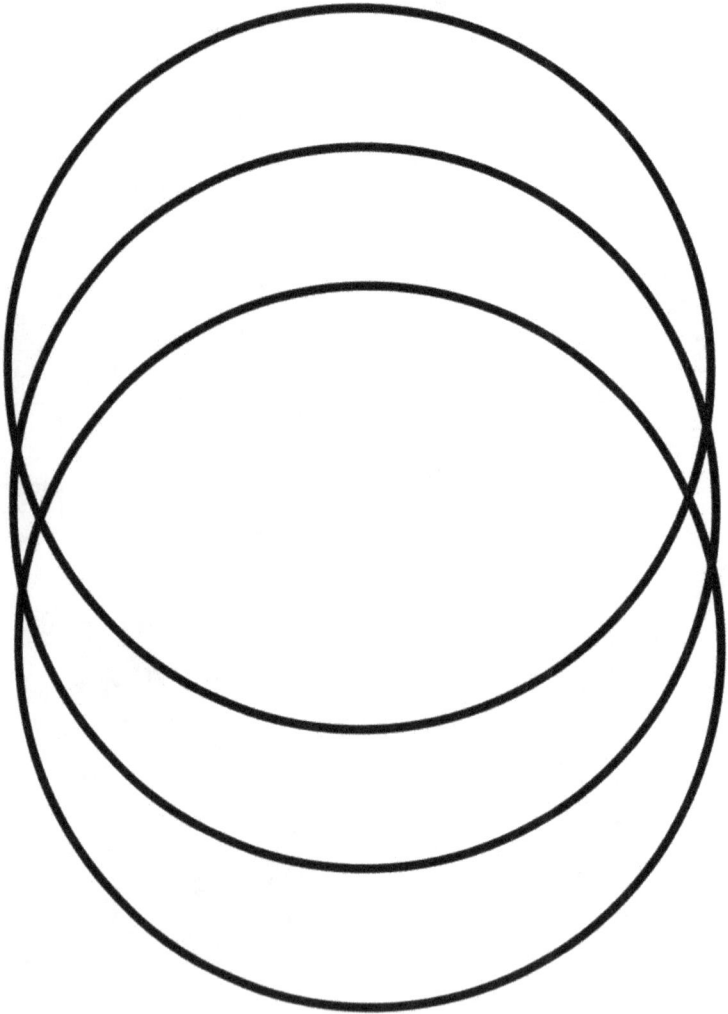

Colour in this line drawing <u>only using</u> **shades of pink.**

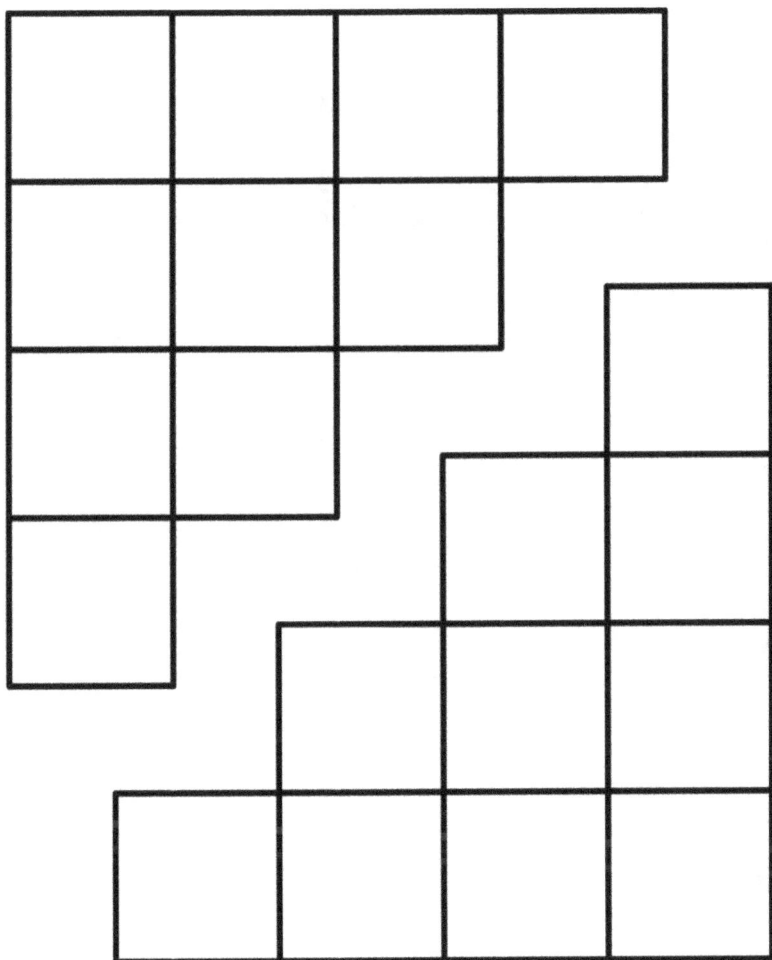

Colour in this line drawing
only using **shades of green.**

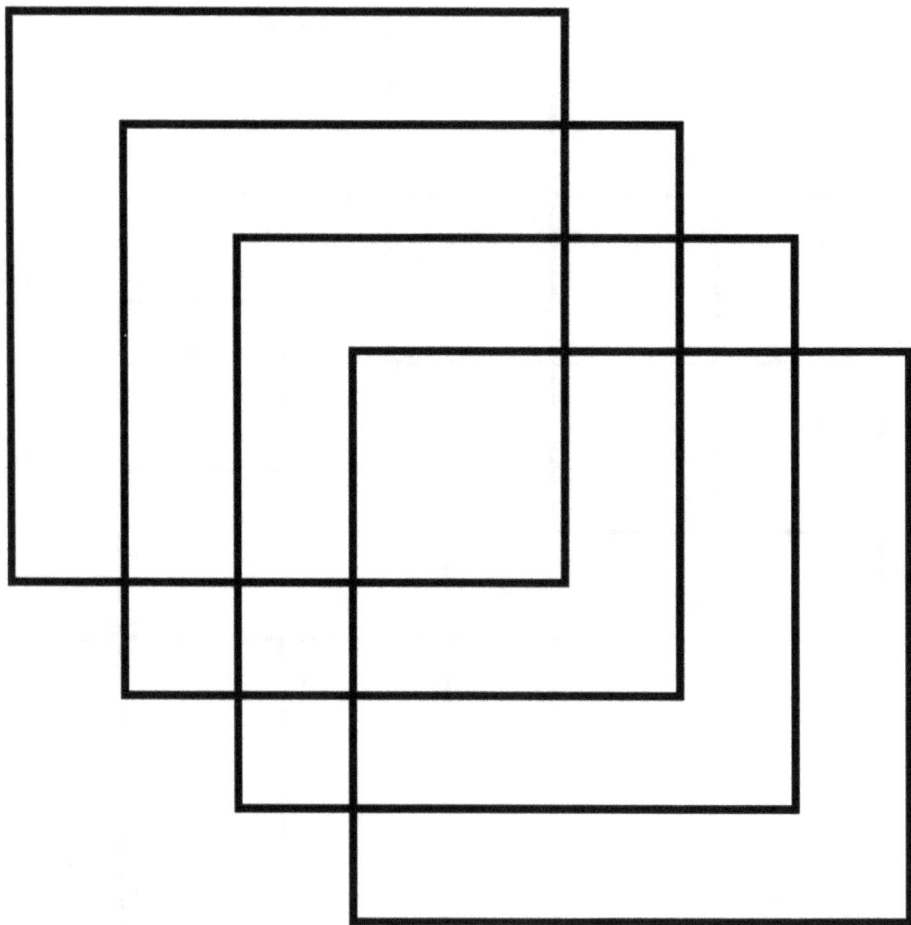

COLOUR TO CALM

Colour in this line drawing _only using_ **shades of blue.**

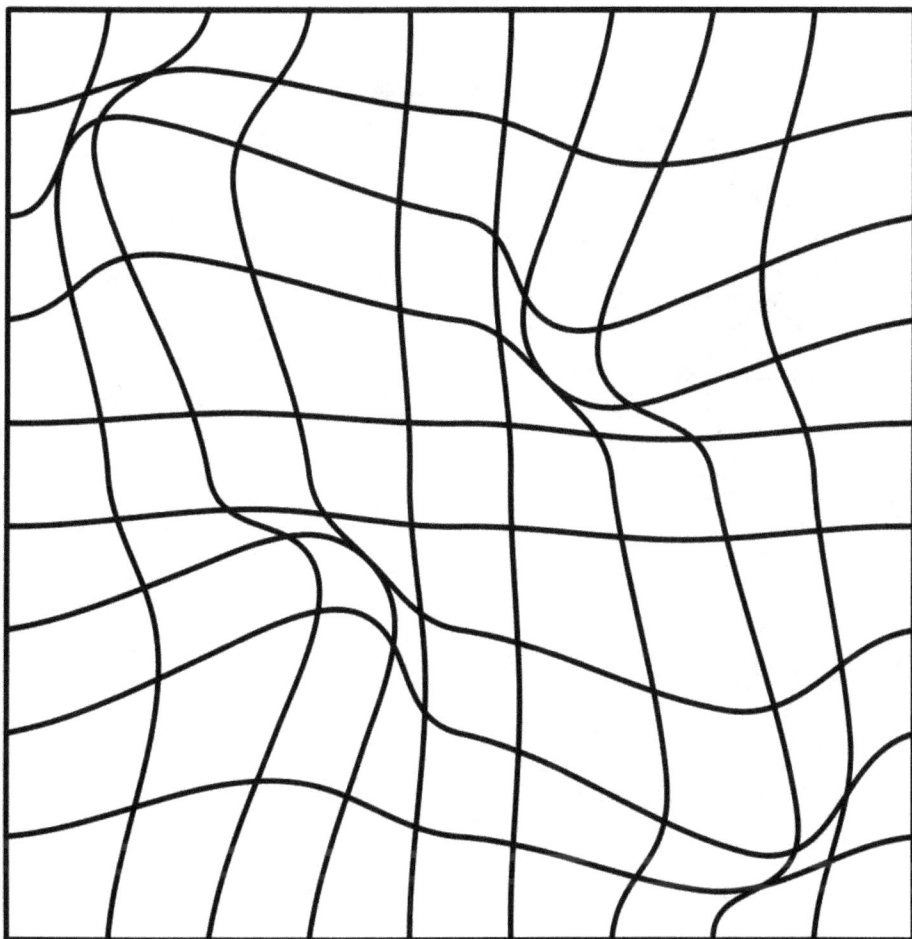

Colour in this line drawing only using shades of red.

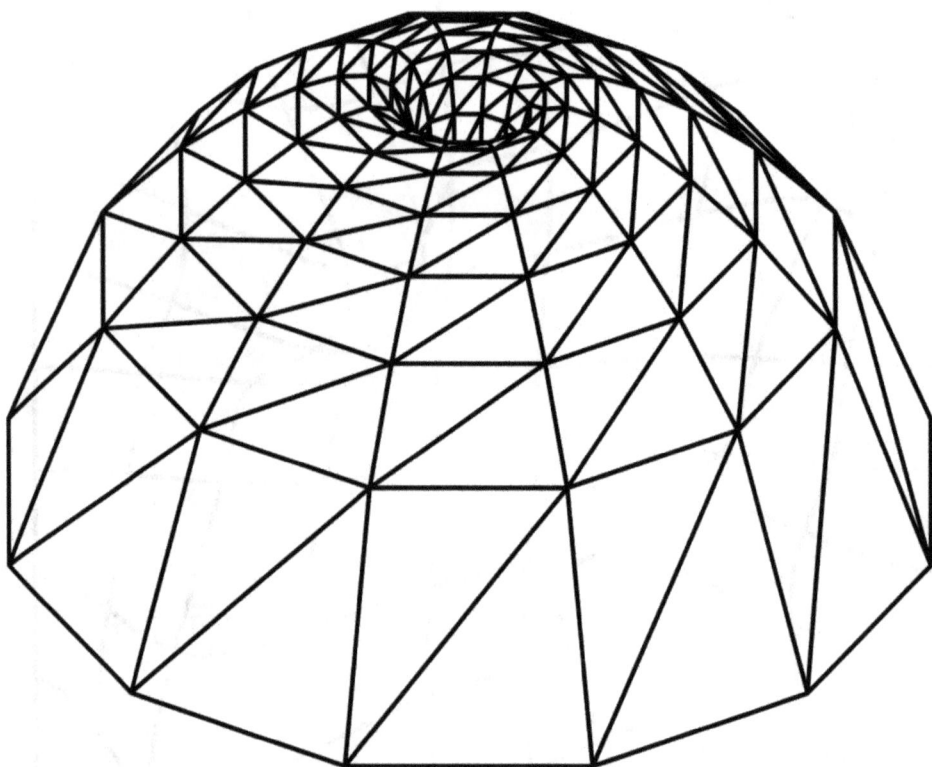

Colour in this line drawing
only using <u>shades of orange.</u>

Symmetry stress-relief

Stressed? Try this!

Dr. Tamara Rosier explains that ADHD brains are prone to an over-emphasis on divergent thinking over convergent thinking. Divergent thinking is highly inventive, and develops in several different directions at once, at a prolific rate. While it's a creative way to make sure our brains are stimulated, divergent thinking is exhausting day-in and day-out. Try these symmetry tracing exercises to activate your convergent thinking brain, and flex that muscle so you can switch more frequently between both types of thinking. The symmetry element subconsciously reinforces the idea of balanc

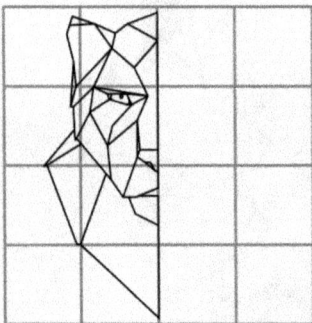

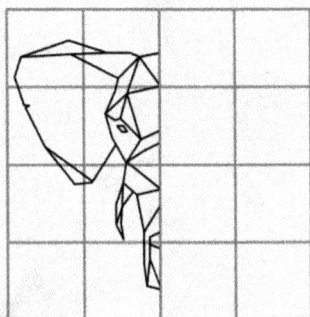

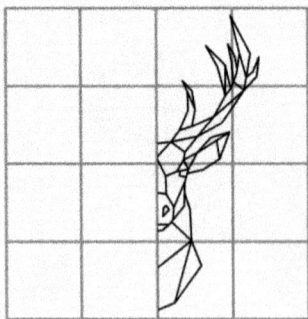

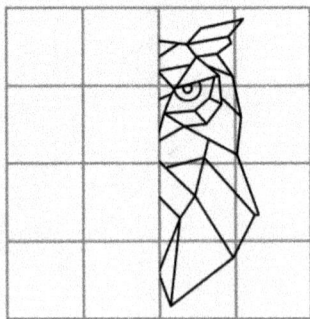

Complete the animal's face using the grid for symmetry. Colour if you desire.

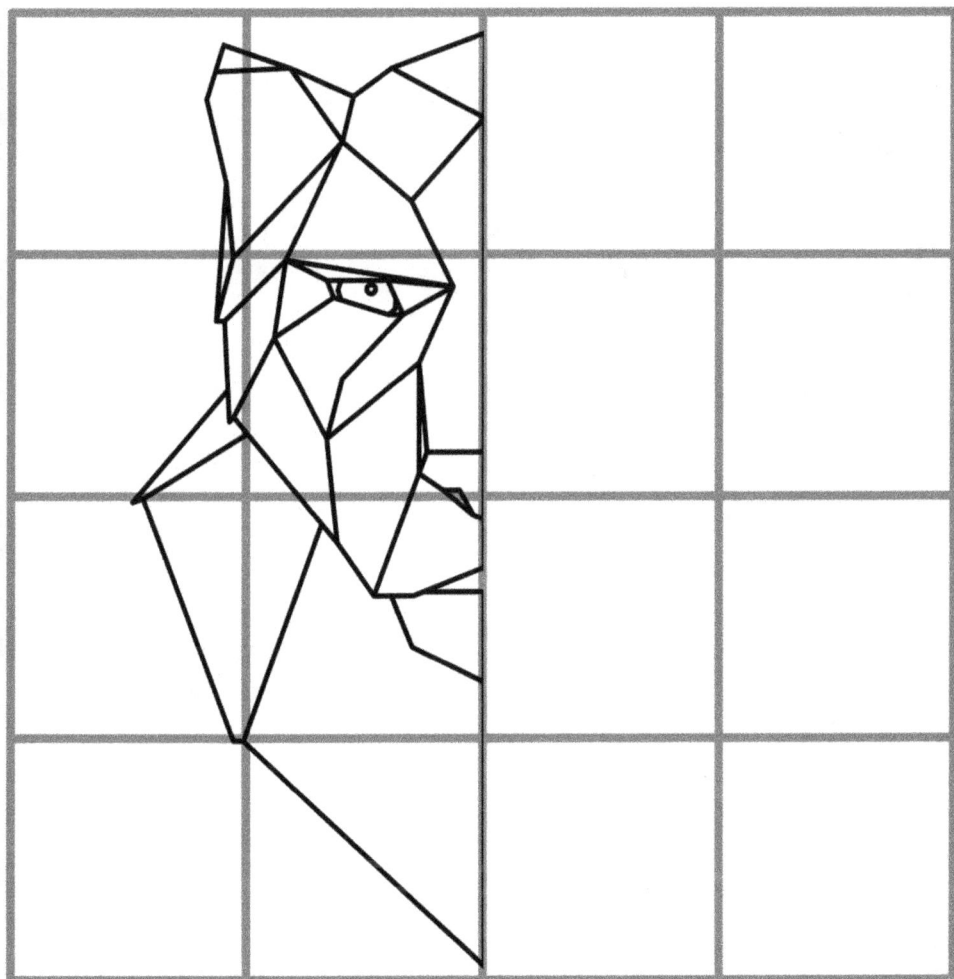

Complete the animal's face using the grid for symmetry. Colour if you desire.

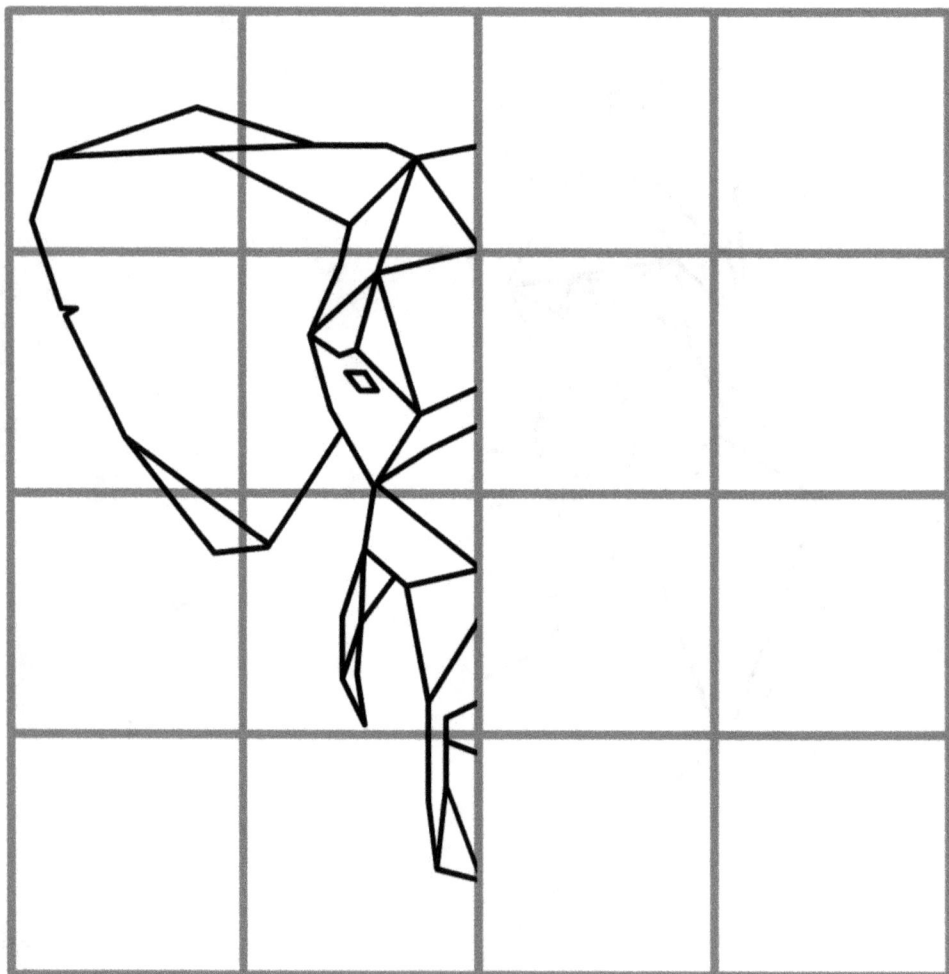

Complete the animal's face using the
grid for symmetry. Colour if you desire.

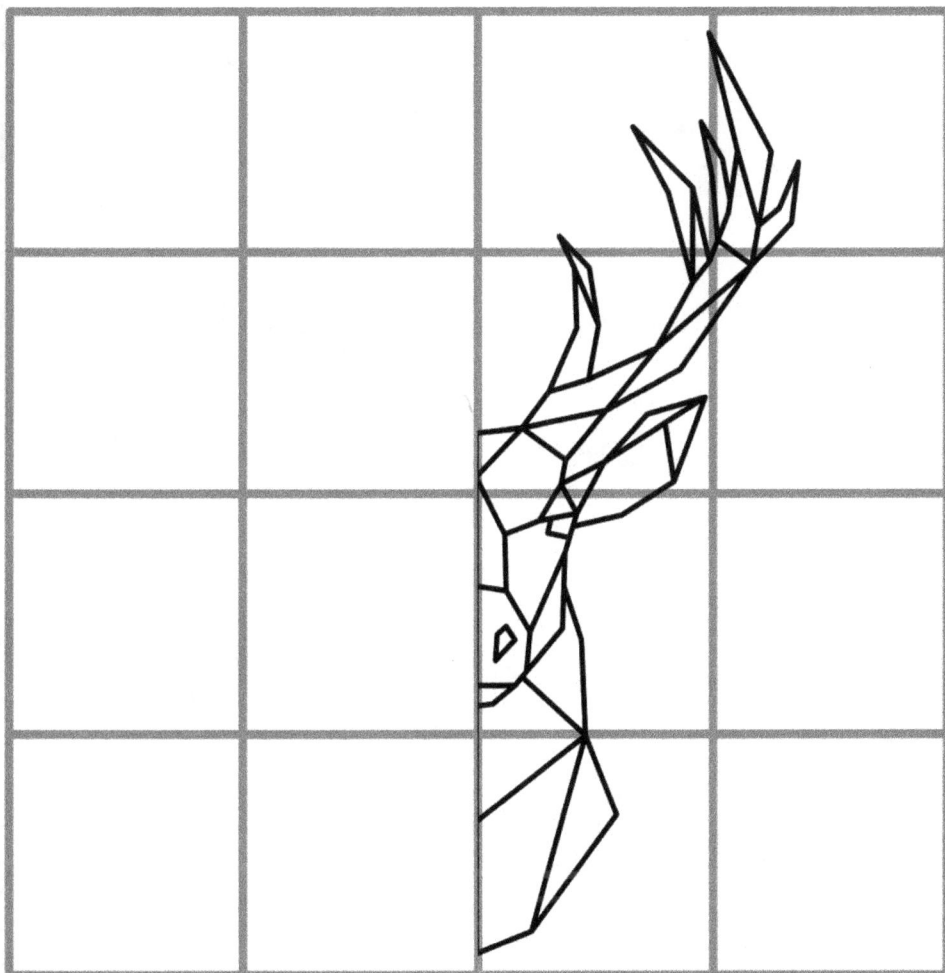

Complete the animal's face using the grid for symmetry. Colour if you desire.

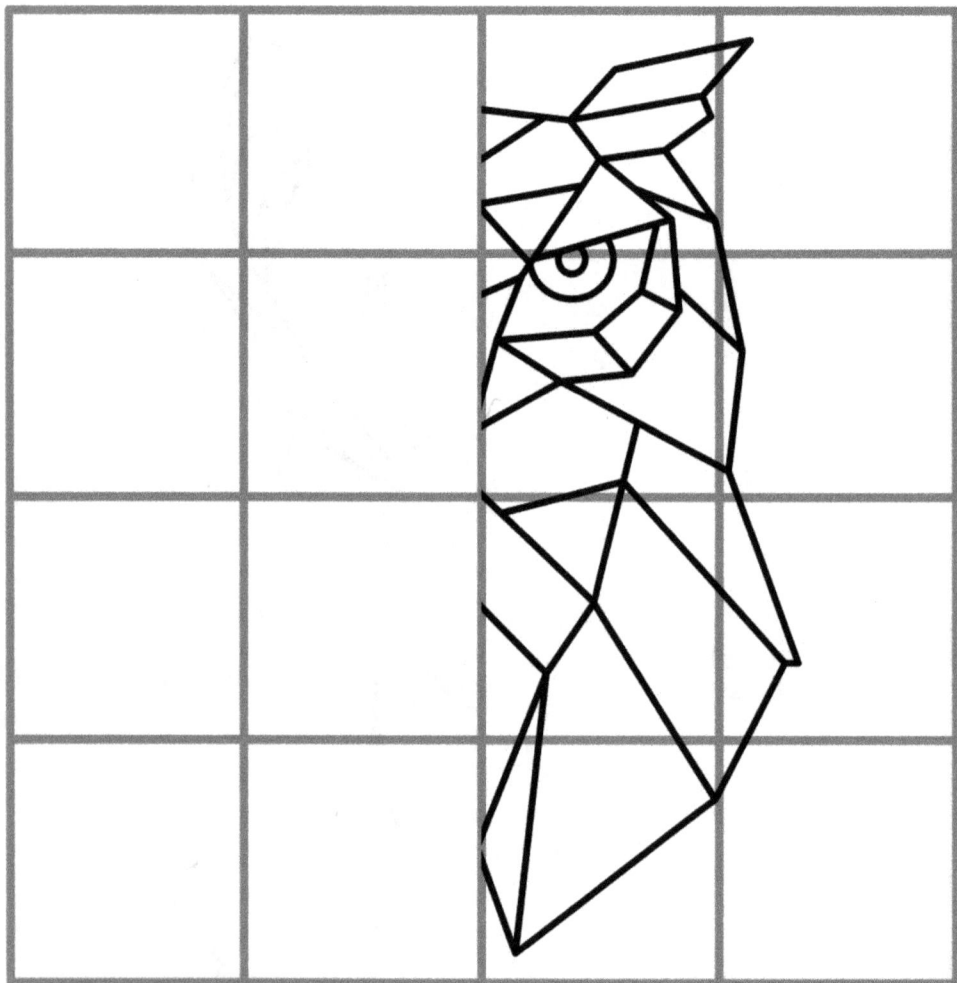

Mini calm moments

I've also included smaller versions you can print onto card, and keep in your wallet, purse, or laptop bag - handy in meetings or moments of stress, where you can duck into the toilet and calm your mind with these exercises.

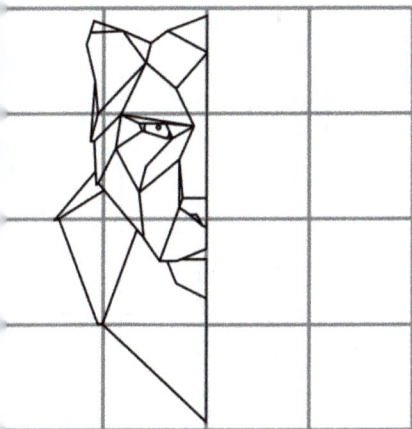

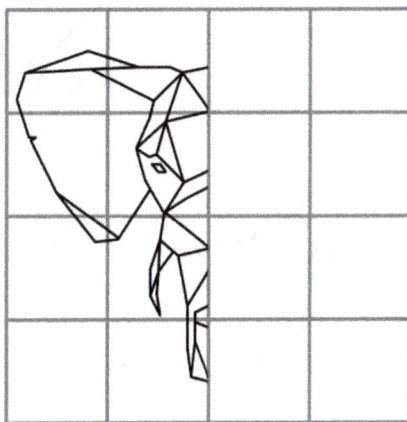

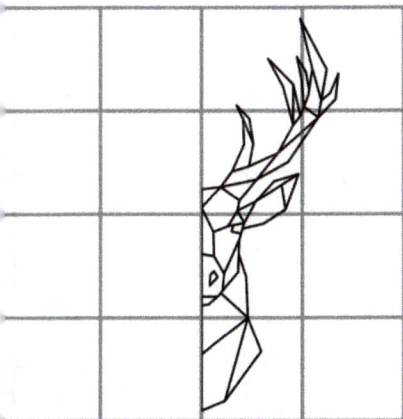

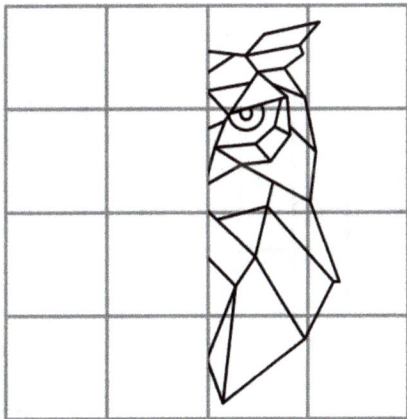

Print page on thicker card

✂ - - - - - - - - - - - - - - - -

 only shades of **yellow**

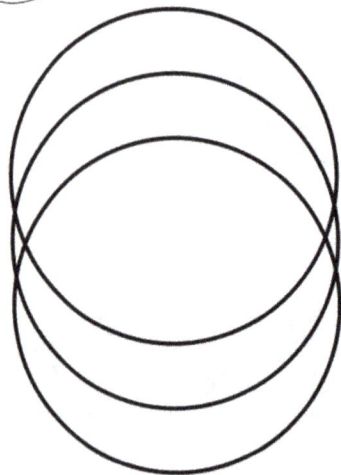

 only shades of **pink**

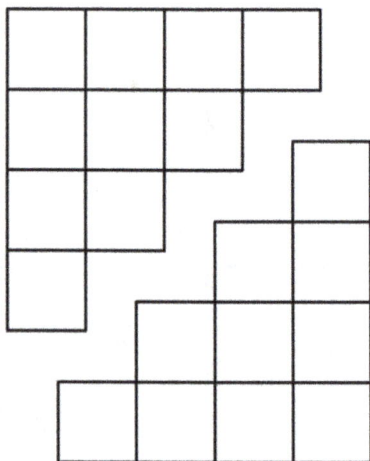

 only shades of **green**

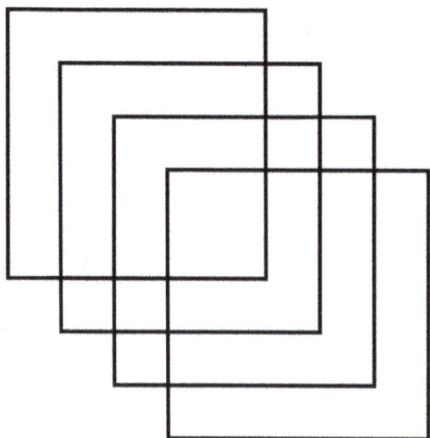

 only shades of **blue**

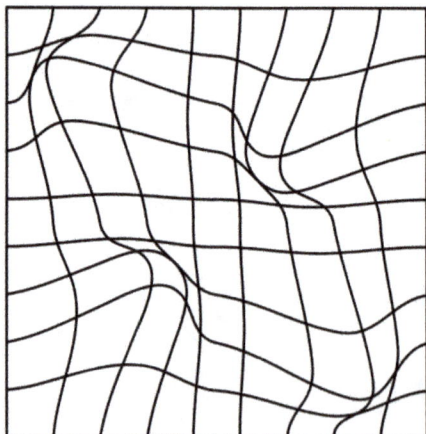

Brain dump + journal

🖉 **In this section:**

Blank monthly brain dump pages for Jan-Dec

- Brain dump - layout variations
- lined
- bullet journal
- grid
- checklist
- blank

Journal section (duplicate as needed)

tips & how it works

Brain dump
+ journal

How to use:

✓

Use these brain dump & journal templates to get those whizzing thoughts out of your head and onto the page.

✓

Our templates include monthly brain dumps to categorise and find ideas easily later, and multiple layout options including lined, bullet journal, grid, checklist and blank. Find what works for you or mix it up!

The science bits

ADHD NEUROLOGICAL TRAIT	OUR PLANNER DESIGN
DELUGE OF CONSTANT THOUGHTS PINGING IN OUR BRAIN LEADING TO OVERWHELM AND FORGETFULNESS	BRAIN DUMP PAGES WITH MULTIPLE LAYOUTS - LINED, GRID, CHECKLIST, BULLET JOURNAL AND BLANK PAGES
PREFERENCE FOR DIVERGENT (HIGHLY CREATIVE) THINKING AND AVERSION/APATHY TOWARDS CONVERGENT (LOGICAL, CATEGORICAL) THINKING	CONVERGENCE-MODIFIED BRAIN DUMPS FOR EACH MONTH OF THE YEAR, SO YOU CAN EASILY CATEGORISE AND FIND IDEAS BY EACH MONTH

January
BRAIN DUMP

MON TUE WED THU FRI SAT

SUN

○   ○   ○   ○   ○   ○   ○

YEAR:

February
BRAIN DUMP

MON TUE WED THU FRI SAT SUN

○   ○   ○   ○   ○   ○   ○

YEAR:

March

BRAIN DUMP

MON TUE WED THU FRI SAT

○ ○ ○ ○ ○ ○ SUN ○

YEAR:

April
BRAIN DUMP

MON TUE WED THU

FRI SAT SUN

○ ○ ○ ○ ○ ○ ○

YEAR:

May

BRAIN DUMP

MON TUE WED THU

FRI SAT SUN

◯ ◯ ◯ ◯ ◯ ◯ ◯

YEAR:

June

BRAIN DUMP

MON TUE WED THU

FRI SAT SUN

○　○　○　○　○　○　○

YEAR:

July
BRAIN DUMP

MON TUE WED THU

FRI SAT SUN

○   ○   ○   ○   ○   ○   ○

YEAR:

August
BRAIN DUMP

MON TUE WED THU FRI SAT

SUN

○ ○ ○ ○ ○ ○ ○

YEAR:

September
BRAIN DUMP

MON TUE WED THU FRI SAT SUN

○ ○ ○ ○ ○ ○ ○

YEAR:

October
BRAIN DUMP

MON TUE WED THU FRI SAT SUN

○ ○ ○ ○ ○ ○ ○

YEAR:

November
BRAIN DUMP

MON TUE WED THU FRI SAT SUN

○   ○   ○   ○   ○   ○   ○

YEAR:

December
BRAIN DUMP

MON TUE WED THU FRI SAT SUN

○ ○ ○ ○ ○ ○ ○

YEAR:

Brain dump

○   ○   ○   ○   ○   ○   ○   DATE:

Brain dump

MON TUE WED THU FRI SAT SUN

○ ○ ○ ○ ○ ○ ○

DATE:

Brain dump

MON TUE WED THU FRI SAT SUN

○ ○ ○ ○ ○ ○ ○

DATE:

Brain dump

MON TUE WED THU FRI SAT SUN

○   ○   ○   ○   ○   ○   ○

DATE:

Brain dump

MON TUE WED THU FRI SAT SUN

○　　○　　○　　○　　○　　○　　○

DATE:

Journal